InSide the Cubicle

*Laugh.
Every day!*

— Dave

Laugh
Every Day
!

Ava
1/4/19

InSide the Cubicle

Discover What *Really* Affects Workplace Communication and Morale

Dave Fleming

VONCHEEKER$ON
PRESS

Voncheeker$on Press
Inside the Cubicle: Discover What *Really* Affects Workplace Communication and Morale
Dave Fleming

Copyright © 2013 by Dave Fleming
All Rights Reserved

Cover Design: Steve Plummer

All Rights Reserved. This book was self-published by the author Dave Fleming under Voncheeker$on Press. No part of this book may be reproduced in any form by any means without the express permission of the author. This includes reprints, excerpts, photocopying, recording, or any future means of reproducing text.

If you would like to do any of the above, please seek permission first by contacting the author at dave@daveflemingspeaks.com.

Published in the United States by Voncheeker$on Press

ISBN: 978-0615887609

Printed by CreateSpace, aDBA of On-Demand Publishing, LLC

Happy are those who dream dreams and are ready to pay the price to make them come true.

LEON J. SUENES

Thank you to my family (especially LDF) and friends who helped me and pushed me to deliver on this quote.

ABOUT THE AUTHOR

The only place success comes before work is in the dictionary.
VINCE LOMBARDI

Would I rather be feared or loved? Easy, both. I want people to be afraid of how much they love me.
MICHAEL SCOTT, DUNDER MIFFLIN REGIONAL MANAGER

Dave Fleming is one of the top speakers and corporate trainers in the country. He is a workplace expert committed to helping individuals and companies improve communication, increase collaboration, and boost morale.

He's also funny. He was voted the number two corporate comedian in America by CBSNews.com. Previously, he worked in marketing for companies like Pizza Hut and Dr Pepper. He has a BS in Marketing from Miami University.

Find out more about Dave at www.daveflemingspeaks.com.

CONTENTS

Preface 11
How To Read This Book 15

THE MORNING ROUTINE 19
  1 Rise 'n' Shine 21
  2 The Curse of the Storyteller 27
  3 The Most Important Room of All: The Break Room . . . 29

THE IMPACT OF THE MACHINES 33
  4 The Copier Dilemma. 35
  5 The Triangular-Shaped SUPER PHONE 39
  6 The Conference Call From Home 43
  7 Voice Mail Recording Sessions 45
  8 E-Mailing It 47
  9 All of the Wonders of the Internet 53

MEETINGS 59
  10 The Double-Booked Calendar 61
  11 Weekly Meetings, Weekly Challenges. 65
  12 Big Meetings, Big Audiences, Big Issues 71
  13 National Sales Meeting. 77

THE BOSS 89
  14 Sunday Night & Monday Morning Stress 91
  15 The Arrival Plan That Avoids The Boss 95
  16 The Power of the Boss's Involvement 99
  17 The Corporate Offsite 103

18 The Important Documents 109

HALLWAYS AND BATHROOMS AND CUBES, OH MY . . 113

19 Hallway Chatter. 115

20 Put My Focus in [Brackets] 123

21 Trust & Respect. 127

22 Most-of-a-Cube 133

FOOD FIGHTS 139

23 The Hunger Games 141

24 Birthdays Make Us Act Like Whos 145

MY CAREER 147

25 A President Practices Passion. 149

26 A Strong First Impression 153

27 May the Force Be With Me 155

28 The Merger of Marketing and Humor. 159

29 Find the Right Recognition 163

30 The Road to this Book 167

The Final Cube Tip 171

PREFACE

Conference calls are funny. Really, they are. If you look at them the way I do, from the INSIDE. That is my goal, to help you go INSIDE. Inside the mindset of people at work. Inside the decisions they make about food, about clothing choices, about words they say.

You see, while everyone is trying to be really good at the jobs they were hired to do, they are battling all of these other things all day long. Understanding these real issues is a critical component of morale, and it will certainly help you be more productive, improve your communication, and allow you more time to excel in your job—I guarantee it.

I'm talking about the real stuff we encounter every day: our obsession with wearing denim to work, the joy of finding brownies on the break room table, or sneaking to one's desk when getting to work late. This book addresses the things everyone inside a cubicle is thinking about but never really talks about.

So what makes me the expert on this material? I've worked in corporate America for over 20 years. OK, big deal, lots of people have worked in corporate jobs. I acknowledge that, but I see the office environment differently than most. I break down the cubicle world the way Jerry Seinfeld examines air travel, Halloween, or scuba diving—I get deep into the minutiae. These observations are real for a company of 10 people or 10,010.

But at the same time, I want to make it BETTER. The office can be so much more rewarding. But, good lord, let's stop taking ourselves so seriously and take a minute to laugh at the things we all do each day. Enough with the passive aggressive notes on the break room fridge. And when we have the chance to make little changes that benefit everyone we have to do it. So each chapter ends with Cube Tips that are suggestions and interpretations of human behavior that you can implement the second after you read it.

One quick example for you: 67% of people say they have rifled through the box lunches at a corporate meeting looking for one that had a chocolate chip cookie in it. This is what's real. This is what is distracting people from delivering their KPIs (acronyms are ridiculous, but we'll get to those later). Everyone wants the chocolate chip cookie. And they are tearing through perfectly put together box lunches looking for it. And some of them will go back to their seats, beaming that they found one, finish the sandwich and the chips, remove the cellophane covering the cookie and discover, to their horror, that they actually grabbed an oatmeal raisin cookie disguised as a chocolate chip—that situation can ruin a perfectly good work day.

Here's your first, simple lesson to make your office experience more rewarding and instantly improve morale: All BOX LUNCHES, no matter the event or meeting, GET CHOCOLATE CHIP COOKIES. It's easier to order them this way. Your people aren't digging through all of them and everybody gets the number one, preferred cookie. And as an aside to any and all box lunch builders and providers, can you kindly put the condiments on the side in little packets? Let me control the ratios because maybe I want to ignore the dressings 100%. Thanks. Love, Dave.

The layout of the book is simple—I am going to take you inside the mind of what people think in a variety of work-related situations (some of which actually happen at home). I hope you laugh a lot. But, I hope you also gain a lot of wisdom from my observations and implement some (OK, in all transparency, I'm hoping all) of my suggestions to make your office so much more rewarding.

Finally, I thank you for buying this book. And if you want my point of view on your office dilemma, e-mail me at dave@daveflemingspeaks.com. Or send me a funny picture from your office. Laughter is the greatest.

HOW TO READ THIS BOOK

Each section represents a part of workplace life that is full of distractions that challenge communication, morale, and ultimately, productivity. It may be the machines, the meetings, or just the way the "human" resources interact with each other. Each chapter is a subset of that section. Some chapters cover several topics, some cover just one.

I will then take you INSIDE each issue. I will literally helicopter you right into a workplace situation and you will watch it unfold. You will see how people behave and react. As I said before, everyone wants to be good at their job, but it is a LOT harder than it looks because of all of the other stuff that gets in the way. I'm going to help you see what we are all confronting and suggest ways to make it better.

These suggestions are called "Cube Tips." They are my recommendations that can make an immediate impact on communication and morale in your office.

There are a few parts of the book called "Oh the Things We Say (or Do)" sprinkled throughout the sections. These are simply funny observations that outline specific workplace behavior that should be instantly recognizable to you.

Finally, if you come across this acronym *BHT, you will have arrived at a "Big Honkin' Tangent." These tangents are humorous anecdotes, opinions, and observations that I added to a specific topic.

InSide the Cubicle

Discover What *Really* Affects Workplace Communication and Morale

Dave Fleming

THE MORNING ROUTINE

The workday starts with you being jarred awake by either a horrible buzzer or the music of your favorite station. You can delay work in seven-minute increments if you like by pounding on the snooze button. Or you can grab your iPhone and get the work started without even leaving your bed. Regardless, we all have a morning routine.

That morning routine also features the massive dilemma that is choosing an outfit for work. And even when you arrive at the office, the path from your car to your desk to get work started is fraught with challenge

Think about your routine…I bet it is pretty similar every single day. The routine feels comfortable. But inside the routine, there are decisions and distractions that affect morale, affect communication, and ultimately affect your productivity for the day.

CHAPTER 1

RISE 'N' SHINE

THE SMART PHONE ON THE NIGHT STAND

Workplace communication can actually start the minute you wake up in the morning. Because electronic communication never stops—e-mails, texts, tweets, and Facebook posts keep coming in. People with a smart phone never leave the office—it's just a matter of whether they choose to turn it on or not. Let's go INSIDE…

Look at Brad, right there, fast asleep. His alarm is about to startle him awake at 6:04. (BHT: Why do we set our alarms for these strange times, like 6:04?) Brad is a bit of a workaholic, extremely paranoid, and quite frankly, addicted to his iPhone. He will not allow it to be more than three feet from him at any time. If you look really closely, you can see it sitting there on his nightstand. When Brad charges his iPhone overnight, it has to be on the nightstand next to his bed.

Brad knows that each morning work will be waiting for him on his smart phone. Work just sits there, like an obedient golden retriever, waiting for him to interact with it. Work knows Brad will eventually feed it or throw the ball. At least work doesn't slobber, which is good. OK, enough with the dog analogy.

Since Brad's smart phone is on the nightstand, he can start the communication process the second he rises in the morning because he doesn't want to miss anything. If something BIG is going down this morning, he's got to know. Brad's alarm goes off; he smacks the alarm clock, HARD, three times, finally finding the snooze button. Twenty-one minutes later, after this exact act is played out three more times, in perfect seven-minute snooze increments, Brad gets up.

He immediately grabs his iPhone and is ready to discover what work he might be the second to know about. The challenge is he has to wade through 17 Groupons and other e-mail solicitations to find a potential work e-mail that rolled in between midnight and 6:00 a.m.

*BHT: What's up with the Groupon people? Why is it 73% off, and why is Brad about to buy carpet cleaning? He didn't need it, but he bought it. Seventy-three percent off. Groupon is a smart communicator—they know we are obsessed for information in the mornings and jam a variety of offers down our throats knowing that one of them is likely to be relevant.

The one thing Brad is hoping to avoid in the morning is the work e-mail with the exclamation point—the RED exclamation point. That piece of communication usually means that the proverbial brown stuff is about to hit the fan. Brad will be at the mercy of the information in that e-mail, and it probably has the world's worst acronym tied to it, too: ASAP.

ASAP allegedly means As Soon As Possible. But that's not what it means. It means RFN. Right Freakin' Now (feel free to use the full F-bomb for effect if you like). As Soon As Possible on the surface sounds like you can fit it in whenever it is convenient for you. That is not the case. ASAP means RFN.

On this morning, no exclamation points or any other work fire drills are there to greet him in text or e-mail form. He can carry on with his normal morning routine. *BHT: What happens when there is a significant work issue over at the fire station? A fire drill REALLY IS an actual a fire drill.

C_uB_e T_iP_s

That smart phone is powerful, insanely addictive, and constantly trying to communicate with us, so be careful. Don't be that lame dad that is "playing" with his kids on the playground as he types an e-mail while pushing his daughter on the swings. Companies and managers can feed this addiction and create scenes like this. People will be as addicted to the device as they are expected to be. Most companies are not 911—let's establish some work/life balance and provide answers in the morning, not at 11:00 p.m. While the smart phone is a smart choice on the road, it is a very dumb choice at the family dinner table (and will absolutely affect workplace morale if it impacts a happy family life).

Finally, I would be remiss if I did not point out that every office does have the exclamation point e-mail abuser. This person thinks he or she is more important than everybody else, by throwing around the exclamation point like bread at the duck pond. Unfortunately for these people, they become the boy that cried exclamation point. The one day they really need something RFN, no one will believe them.

THE QUEST FOR THE PERFECT WORK OUTFIT

We communicate with our work colleagues in a lot of ways. Some are obvious: we talk to them, we e-mail them, or we send them a text. Others are not quite as obvious: the way we decorate our

Cube Tips

Wardrobe does say a lot about the people in your office. Most guys slap on a blue button-down and some slacks and are good to go. The fairer sex has more choices and more opportunities to show personal style. But guys, girls, the neat, and the slovenly all agree on one fashion choice that is one of the biggest workplace morale boosters of all: denim.

Everybody loves wearing jeans to work. It's like when the elementary school class that brought in the most canned goods and won the ice cream party. WE LOVE WEARING JEANS TO WORK.

Some offices have casual Fridays. And sometimes, companies will allow "BONUS" jeans days on a Tuesday if you make a donation to a certain cause. This situation always has two distinct groups of people. The first group heard you could pay five bucks to wear jeans, did not care about the name of the cause, and reveled in the freedom of wearing denim on a Tuesday. The second group is comprised of the folks that hop out of their cars in their typical business attire and see a sea of jeans all around them: Levis, Wranglers, button fly, fly is down, skinny, not-so-skinny, it doesn't matter—everyone else is in jeans. Morale shot.

Don't mess up a BONUS Jeans Day Tuesday; it can hurt and instantly destroy morale. People are simply unable to work around denim-clad coworkers when they miss out. Free bonus tip: put FREE JEANS on your calendar and send a group text the night before to remind everyone in your work group or team. Better yet, throw a spare pair in the backseat of your car so you never, ever miss.

Everyone feels liberated when they get to put on their favorite pair of jeans and head to work. It's an easy, no-cost benefit to reward good work, support a cause, or just improve your office morale. If you individually don't have the authority to approve company-wide jeans, then push for your department or your team to have that benefit (tie it to great sales results or the completion of a long project). Identify a cause your team is passionate about, and you win on multiple levels. I promise you this: if you find multiple ways throughout the year to unleash denim in your office, your team's morale will soar.

Chapter 2

THE CURSE OF THE STORYTELLER

Getting off to a good start on a work morning can be critical to a productive workday. We all have our little routines. Some people need a cup of coffee. Some people ease in by reviewing e-mails. Others prefer to make lists for the day and get great satisfaction by crossing off items throughout the day. (First item on the list: "make a list"). Having this process interrupted in any way can impact morale and productivity. Let's go INSIDE…

Here we are in the parking garage at Lisa's office. She has had a challenging commute battling stop-and-go traffic and now she desires a little peace and quiet. As the famous proverb says: "Silence is golden." This is a case when the best communication is no communication at all. For the short time and distance from her car to her desk, she would like to make a solo trek. She wants the world to deliver its part of that proverb. Sometimes, despite her best intentions, that wish is destroyed by the storyteller.

The storyteller scene usually plays out the same way. It starts with surprise…just as Lisa is getting out of her car and comes around the corner, undetected, "The Storyteller" approaches (and Lisa is now trapped). Nothing is more debilitating than the storyteller approaching. These are the people, and you know them well, who tell you facts about their lives that should not be shared publicly anywhere. And now Lisa knows she has a front row seat for the next three minutes until she gets to her desk.

Lisa is a veteran. She knows that when the storyteller approaches, she must take evasive action. She must make up an excuse to get something, anything (a Tic Tac qualifies as a critical item forgotten in haste this morning) from her car. She knows her morale is 100% correlated to her ability to dodge a poodle story from the resident storyteller.

CuBe TiPs

Don't think for a minute that your colleagues don't know who the resident bards are. Be cordial. Be a good teammate. But if it makes your life better, go get that critical paper clip you left in the cup holder of your foreign or domestic vehicle (it's cool, and while you are being rude, you really aren't).

Chapter 3

THE MOST IMPORTANT ROOM OF ALL: THE BREAK ROOM

There are so many rooms where critical communication takes place. But there is one room in particular where every conceivable form is on unique display. Passive-aggressive notes. Personal calls on personal cell phones. Threats. Laughter. Delicacies shared for all. "Delicacies" only a few would even consider touching. The break room has it all. And it is absolutely the only room that nearly every employee goes into EVERY day. It easily has the biggest impact on the office.

Picture the break room in your office—is it the harbinger for morale? I bet if everything is going well in the break room, then life is likely pretty good out in the cubes. But, if you have notes flying and poor microwave behavior, then this room is a culture concern. Let's go INSIDE…

Here we are in the break room—Matt's first stop before he reaches his desk in the morning. The first challenge of his workday is to find safe lodging for his lunch. That sounds pretty easy, but he knows that the break room fridge is teeming with thieves. And he knows that the fridge vultures may steal anything he puts in the fridge without a name on it.

This fridge stress is sad, but Matt must think about it every day. As he is about to put an apple into the fridge, he realizes it cannot sit in there unmarked, by itself. It's ridiculous that he has to unearth a red Sharpie and write his name in big, bold print on a piece of masking tape and attach that to the apple and then, and only then, is it safe for him to put that apple in the fridge.

The break room fridge is also home to some of the funniest (but not meant to be funny) passive-aggressive notes in the world. Matt's colleagues are clearly paranoid that their lunch will be stolen, their dairy creamer will be used, or their Thin Mints will be eaten. So notes are taped to these items. And time is spent writing and taping these notes to the items. Find an office without these notes and you will find trust. And a team that trusts each other in the break room is a team that is going to win in business. Period.

Ironically, just three feet away from the break room fridge is the break room table. It is a communication mechanism of a different sort. It's the communal trough. Anyone can graze on the items that are placed there for the willing masses.

Unfortunately, anyone who has grazed here often regrets eating items like pizza crusts, pink donuts, and the lettuce that the deli meats were sitting on. Matt takes a quick glance at the table in hopes of a Dunkin' Donut munchkin or Chick-fil-A chicken mini, but no such luck—just a fourth of an onion bagel is on the current menu.

Matt has put absolutely disgusting stuff on this table in the past and knows that all items, including this quarter of a bagel, will disappear in seconds. Some of his colleagues actually schedule hourly afternoon reconnaissance missions to make sure a brownie from a poorly attended office baby shower isn't missed. Yes, the break room is the ultimate tease…and distraction.

Matt failed to retrieve his lunch in the break room by 11:45, and he knows he has made a big mistake. At noon, the break room is one of the most noxious places on earth. A perfume made of the smells from the local zoo's skunk exhibit would be an upgrade over the nasal combo platter put together at lunch in the break room. Many of these items reek at room temperature. But when these foods, especially those with fish as a primary ingredient, are tossed into the microwave, it's truly game over.

Matt takes a deep breath and heads into the break room wishing he were wearing a government-issued gas mask. Today's stench concoction is worse than ever as tuna is clearly involved. He quickly finds his lunch and his apple that says "Matt." Unfortunately for Matt, he was late today. And his badge for his late arrival is having that break room stench draped on him like a cloak of cigars after a night at a smoky bar.

CuBe TiPs

Stop the threats, stop the thieves, stop the madness, and help the people. People are spending *way* too much time worrying about the safety of the lunch they brought from home. Don't let the fridge burglars rule this room. Establish rules and all break room visitors will act like adults (and if they don't, revoke privileges—it's that simple).

Next, instead of watching your coworkers wear a path in the carpet to the break room hoping for goodies, bring in your own "afternoon treat jar" and have your team take turns filling it. It sounds simple, but knowing a Kit Kat is around the corner (or go healthy and bring in some nuts or fresh fruit) can be the perfect little push to get through a tough afternoon project.

And, finally, do not let people bring their stench-carrying items into public areas (e.g., no one is eating fish, especially freshly microwaved fish, at their desk). Tuna and burned popcorn kill morale. Period.

THE IMPACT OF THE MACHINES

If you work in a traditional office, you are counting on machines to be effective in your job. And these machines are everywhere. You need that copier to step up and make beautiful copies for the big meeting—no time for a jam. You need that projector to present your slideshow perfectly on the screen, with zero distractions and no reason to call the AV guy. You need your laptop for e-mail and the Internet.

You probably weren't trained on any of the machines you use every day. In fact, you probably take them for granted. Rarely does anyone say, "Wow, that projector is great—my presentation looked beautiful today." If the machines aren't working, your workday can careen out of control. Corral the machines to guarantee great communication and eliminate hits on morale.

Chapter 4

THE COPIER DILEMMA

The copier is probably the largest machine most people utilize in their work lives. It's big. It appears to be fun because of the size of the machine, the moving parts, and the numerous buttons, but it is fraught with potential disaster. But first, let's take a minute—go ahead, do your best Rob Schneider SNL impression, "May-ken cop-eez." Let's go INSIDE...

Brent has a big meeting coming up later today and is heading into the copy room to make copies of his presentation. He puts his originals in the top and peers into that little screen and starts punching buttons. Today, he's clearly feeling a little cocky, so despite the insane degree of difficulty, he has decided to collate AND staple. But trying to figure out which side he wants for the staple is an impossible task. If he wants it in the upper left, no matter what corner he picks on the little screen, it always ends up in the lower right. And then it takes him 10 minutes to remove the staples because he has to find that those little jaws of life hiding in a drawer in the copy room.

But he's going for it; he chooses a corner for his staple, punches in his desire for 15 copies, hits the green start button, takes one step back, and he's making copies. At the beginning it is a beautiful symphony of great sounds...until the whole operation grinds to a halt. Ruh Roh Rastro.

When Brent peers back into that screen (that used to be so friendly), there is now a diagram of the copier on there, with menacing numbers flashing to indicate the places his copies are currently lodged.

But he has to have these copies for the upcoming meeting and frustration is clearly setting in. So he yanks open the front panel, and an intricate combination of dials and contraptions is revealed. It's like a game of Mouse Trap in there, including the little man that jumps into the pool in the back.

To clear the paper and restart this process, he's going to have to turn one of those ridiculous numbered dials. And just as he is about to turn dial number four, another deterrent arises: there is a sign in bright neon print that says, "CAUTION, HOT SURFACES." As it turns out, there is a bulb HOTTER than the sun sitting one millimeter away from dial number four. If he sticks his arm in there, all of his arm hairs will be singed right off.

So do you know how Brent handles this situation (and let's be honest, so does everyone else)? He looks over both shoulders to see if anyone is watching. Then, he closes the copier's front panel doors, grabs his originals out of the top, and walks away...leaving that problem for somebody else.

CuBe Tips

People are sneaking away from the copier, leaving a mess for the next unsuspecting user of that machine. Unless you have someone in your office that has a master's degree in photocopying, you are stuck like most offices with people who *think* they know how

to use all of the advanced features and make copies. Most don't, but they are very good at **NOT** making copies. Stop these jammers from tiptoeing out of the copy room like a person trying to leave a lame party early. You know it's going to jam. Post the number to call if it does. And let's all move on, without the guilt and the paper trail.

cubes, the way we take notes, the way we schedule meetings, and the way we dress ourselves. Because the way we dress communicates our personal brand, it plays a huge role in our relationship with our coworkers.

Every office has the spectrum: the insanely sharp dresser to the slovenly dresser who is a wrinkled mess. Most of us fall in the middle, so we want to get the dressing ourselves right. Let's go INSIDE…

Here we are at Jessica's home. She is in her clothes closet, and she seems a bit distraught. Jessica is getting sick and tired of dressing for work and on this day in particular, she wished she wore the same uniform every day. Today, she wishes she was from another planet and wore the spandex outfit with a V print EVERY SINGLE DAY—it must be the wave of the future, because that's all they wear.

She has a strong dislike for her clothes closet. She wishfully stares at the hangers, but she knows it's the same stuff day after day, week after week. And she knows people are placing wagers on her wardrobe. She knows her coworkers are saying: "I bet you five bucks Jessica wears black today." Or, "I bet you she wears her Tuesday outfit today."

Jessica wishes one day her closet would magically be made over by one of those shows on one of those cable channels in the 200s that we all stumble upon late at night with an expert who is carrying a sledgehammer for no apparent reason.

Sure, Jessica loves showing off a new outfit or "cute shoes." As a quick BHT, I have never and will never say that, but it is definitely something I've heard the fairer sex say in a very positive tone. When Jessica is rocking a new outfit, it is a big boost to her workday, to her personal brand, and to her overall morale. But that new pair of heels is only new for a short time. Then the closet is back to having the same ol' stuff.

Chapter 5

THE TRIANGULAR-SHAPED SUPER PHONE

People absolutely dread conference calls. They see them as boring, often dysfunctional, and rarely run well. They recognize the need but wish they were better. These ritualistic meetings are a drain on morale and productivity when they are not properly orchestrated. We spend more time in meetings than in any other single work activity. These have to get better, because right now, this process is littered with unproductive acts. As mentioned at the front of this book, they are littered with unintended humor. Let's go INSIDE…

Here we are in a meeting room on the third floor. As people enter the room, they join a group of their coworkers huddled around a table, paying homage to the beloved triangle-shaped SUPER PHONE sitting in the middle of the table. And everybody is in a trance, just staring at it. The SUPER PHONE has incredible, hypnotic powers. People do not make eye contact with each other…oh no, they just stare into the super phone.

Next, there's roll call, it's like everyone is in the army. "Let's find out who's on the call," says call leader Jenny. "Who could be out there? So names start being rattled off. Jenny tries to keep up. "Oh hey, Larry, Steve..." three more names go by. The people who don't get personalized hellos are pissed.

Then, as the group waits for the remainder of the team to join the call, it's small talk time. They must find a topic that everyone can all talk about...silence is not golden, it's uncomfortable. So, they bail to the number one conference call small talk topic—the weather. And for the next five minutes, the group receives a five-day forecast complete with a vivid, color-coded description of the Doppler radar for every metropolitan area represented on the call.

So, the call finally gets started and they encounter their first complainer—monotone Melissa in Montana mumbles: "Can you guys speak up? I can't hear...I can't hear." So call leader Jenny watches her coworkers defy all laws of acceptable hygiene and speak one millimeter from the SUPER PHONE—they are practically drooling on it—so a woman 1,000 miles away can hear a little better.

However, there is a fun part of the call. It happens when someone gets on the call after it actually started. Everyone hears that little BEE BEEP, and then the race is on. And the race is on to see who can say three words faster than anybody else: "Who just joined?" And those three words magically become one. "Whojustjoined? Whojustjoined? Whojustjoined?" They are shouting it out like a mom trying to get a toddler's attention on the playground.

"Who could it be, whose voice is blessing us through the SUPER PHONE? Who joined the call SEVEN MINUTES LATE...Whojustjoined?" It's like they're keeping score; it's unbelievable. It should be Jenny's sole job to find out, but many in the group simply can't help themselves.

If that's not bad enough, call leader Jenny then caters to the latecomers and spends the next five minutes of the call rehashing the first five minutes of information that the group already sat through.

It's easy to see how powerful the Super Phone really is. Jenny clearly does not believe turning it off once will work. So, she is actually turning it off five or six times, then checking for a dial tone, just to make sure that she has indeed, silenced the all-powerful, triangular-shaped super phone.

CuBe TiPs

Conference calls are vital to bringing together teams that work across a diverse geography. But most people would rather do nine hours of algebra than join some conference calls because they are so poorly managed. You must set up conference call protocols: (1) agendas must be sent out before the call; (2) meetings must start on time; (3) no rehashing...if you're late, too bad; (4) after the call, notes are sent out the same day so the first 15 minutes of the *next* call are not spent reviewing the last call. Tight, well-run conference calls will be such a drastic, sudden change that morale will rise from a conference call...yes, morale will rise from a group of people discussing a business issue while gathered around the all-powerful, triangular-shaped Super Phone.

Chapter 6

THE CONFERENCE CALL FROM HOME

Some conference calls are taken away from the office. And many of these are taken from an individual's home. Often, the level of preparation is not what it should be. If not handled properly, this can lead to disaster. Let's go INSIDE…

Roy is a sales veteran. He has always worked out in the field, where the action is. He's not a rookie when it comes to the conference call taken from home. He sees it as an opportunity to multi-task. "I'm not going to be needed on *this* call, he thinks to himself."

In fact, he will take this morning's conference call while wearing pajamas…it's not a *video* conference call. He calls in, enters the participant code, presses the speakerphone button, announces his presence, then presses the mute button. He places the phone in the middle of the kitchen table. He plans on surfing the web and eating some Frosted Mini Wheats during today's call…he sees no chance that his name will come up on the call.

He knows that tiny little mute button is his friend—nothing to hear here. Or is it? Because just as Roy puts another heaping scoop of cereal into his mouth, he thinks he hears his name. No, no way.

Then he hears it again. "Where's Roy, where could he be?" says the call leader.

So, Roy has to dive across the table to take the phone off mute and at that exact moment, the doorbell rings, the dog starts barking, and Roy's elbow knocks the bowl of Mini Wheats to the floor...it is complete chaos. The call is completed interrupted—and the loud bark from Roy's labradoodle Rufus will be remembered for a long time. Everyone else on the phone can picture the scene at Roy's and are glad that it wasn't them. In this case for Roy, multi-tasking actually became zero-tasking in a most humiliating fashion.

CuBe TiPs

There's nothing worse than hearing a colleague get embarrassed on the other end of the line due to a poorly timed package delivery. Encourage everyone in your office to treat a home conference call the same way a conference call is handled at the office. I doubt many people show up in the meeting room at the home office with a bowl of Frosted Mini Wheats and a magazine. And at the very least, encourage them to check that their mute button is fully operational.

Chapter 7

VOICE MAIL RECORDING SESSIONS

You can learn a lot about a person from their outgoing voice mail message, trust me. The more creative, outgoing types leave something memorable. Those committed to their companies will mention a new product or service. The workaholic types will make it short and sweet so they can get back to work. And no matter which person we are talking about, I guarantee it took them several takes to record. Let's go INSIDE…

Larry just got back from vacation and needs to change his outgoing voice mail message. It seems like such a simple task, but it is a lot harder than it looks, and it is incredibly awkward.

First, you have to remember the seven steps it takes to navigate the voice mail system to even get the chance to begin the recording. Larry finally gets there, takes a deep breath, ducks his head down below cube height level, presses the number two, and begins to speak.

But Larry can't get it done in one take, ever. It sucks on his first take. He whispers on his second take. He gets interrupted on the third take. As his frustration mounts, he wonders why his office doesn't provide a recording studio for this task.

Wouldn't it be great if every office had a designated room with the egg carton walls, a thin, circular microphone, a stool, a set of headphones, and a guy on the other side of the glass at the mixing board? Larry would nail it every time—and his outgoing voice mail would sound *so* good.

Cube Tips

Obviously a recording studio is impractical—but so fun. But do not underestimate the message being sent by this message. How you say it, what you say, and the way you say it tells your callers something about you. Keep this in mind, focus, and nail it on your first take.

Chapter 8

E-MAILING IT

Communication is defined as *"the imparting or exchanging of information or news."* The primary form of this in the office is via e-mail. It is quick. It is private. It is everywhere. It never stops. It is sometimes hard to interpret. It is spam. It is important. It is company-wide. It is marked with an exclamation point. It is personal. It is 25 meg for one file attachment, which put you over your inbox limit and now you can't send any more e-mails.

E-mail is all of the above and more. If you handle e-mail communication well, you will be more productive. Period. E-mail does not afford you the chance to provide the all-important non-verbal skills that help provide context when speaking. Tone, gestures, facial expressions; they are all missing in e-mail. Because of this, e-mail is affecting morale every single day, every single hour, every single minute, and every single second that somebody hits "send."

THE THREE-FOOT E-MAIL

The primary form of communication in most offices today is e-mail. Most office workers feel inundated by it and no wonder—nearly 300 billion e-mails are sent each day globally. Each one is full of distractions. Spam, junk, copies, blind copies—all are coming at us all day long. Let's go INSIDE...

Steve loves technology. He is a wizard with the entire Office suite of programs. He texts at 100 mph. He loves electronic communication, but this allows him to be less personable and hide behind his keyboard.

Look at Steve, sitting in his cubicle, typing away. He is writing an e-mail that will travel a grand total of three feet to his left to Jill who is SITTING RIGHT NEXT TO HIM! Steve's less personal style consistently makes it harder for him to influence others when selling his ideas, programs, and vision.

Unfortunately, Steve also takes his e-mail abuse a step further and commits a far worse crime: he overuses the Cc box. This felony played out in the following fashion earlier today: (1) A problem arose on one of Steve's projects. (2) The problem involves multiple people. (3) Project leader Steve replied all to the group and copied his boss and other senior leaders. (4) All other team members are now incensed at Steve because in lieu of providing a solution in the e-mail, he just elevated the issue. (5) Now senior management will be wondering what happened. Moral of the story: NOT GOOD FORM, STEVE—that's why many think the Cc box should be renamed the CYA box.

CuBe TiPs

Add the personal touch back to the office. Encourage your colleagues to actually get out of their cube and visit someone to discuss an issue instead of sending an e-mail that will travel less than thirty feet. You must set the proper example, especially if you are a manager.

And far too many people are hiding behind that dreaded Cc box. These folks decide to copy the entire world on a problem that could have been solved with

one or two phone calls. Don't enable this type of behavior and make a point to provide feedback to your peers when you see it done. Proper communication can build trust and morale. Poor communication, including overuse of the Cc box, can destroy it.

THE RECALL E-MAIL

E-mail presents so many potential challenges because it is "from" a person, but it is impossible to know the true meaning of an e-mail because e-mail does not include nonverbal communication that is a critical part of human interaction. Yes, we can type in all caps, or use exclamation points to get a point across. But the tone of an e-mail can easily be misconstrued as the receiver applies their own lens to the words on their computer, tablet, or smart phone.

And sometimes, people hit send too fast. And then they want that e-mail back. Let's go INSIDE…

Tracy is working on an excel spreadsheet at her desk. She is focused. Suddenly, she is interrupted. On Tracy's laptop screen, a notification pops up that says Brant Johnson would like to recall the e-mail entitled "Montgomery Budget." Her focus is shot.

Well, Brant, here's the reality of this situation. Tracy was not remotely interested in the "Montgomery Budget" e-mail when it first arrived. But now that you want it back, you have changed her interest level significantly. Tracy will now be reading every single word. Tracy wants to know what has gone astray in this e-mail. If this is a clever ploy to get her to read the original e-mail, it's working.

CuBe TiPs

Dear reader, please be sure the recall is absolutely necessary, e.g. a mistake that affects contracts, the law, or a piece of printed material for example. If you just want to change a few words or a color, don't do it. Let your harmless typos or formatting errors go—your recipients might find them, and they very well might not. (They might not even read it!)

The Read Receipt

E-mail communication is full of potential miscommunication. And there are people who are paranoid about the role that other people play in accomplishing their work tasks. So, they don't 100% trust their coworkers. They want to be able to prove that a single person or group of individuals read their e-mail. And this is ticking people off. Let's go INSIDE…

Look at Karen over there. She just opened an e-mail from Lloyd and up pops that most annoying box that says: "The sender has requested a read response." Karen immediately wants to know why Lloyd is checking up on her.

And what if Karen clicks yes to the receipt and opens Lloyd's e-mail but never reads it? Lloyd can say, "I know you read it because I got a read receipt." But the fallacy of the read receipt is that it comes at the *beginning*, not the end, of this e-mail reading transaction. How does the computer really know if Karen read the e-mail?

Because, seconds after opening the e-mail, Karen got a call from somebody in Finance alerting her that two thirds of a chocolate birthday cake was discovered in the break room. She knows that cake might last two minutes tops, because the vultures will be circling. So she sprints to the break room and spends 10 minutes with other cake-munching coworkers. When she gets back to her desk, she is distracted and forgets about Lloyd's e-mail. So, despite saying yes to the receipt, she never read it.

That is why Karen rarely clicks "yes" for a read receipt, because the machine, quite frankly, has no idea. In fact, she finds it quite liberating to move her mouse over that "no" button and click it. Maybe she did read it, maybe she didn't, you'll never know.

C∪BE TIPS

An e-mail with a read receipt can destroy morale, blackball individuals, and create gossipy conversations. Read receipts break trust among coworkers. If you are a manager (and seriously, even if you are not) you cannot, under any circumstances, send an e-mail to any member of your team as a read receipt. Again, if something is so crucial, meet with them in person. Secondly, if you have a coworker that "loves them some e-mail receipts," step in and stop it—they may not realize the damage that little box can do.

THE E-MAIL OVER-FOLLOW UPPER

Sometimes you need somebody else to communicate back to you to finish a project. You either don't have the expertise, the data access, or the information required to finalize it. Let's go INSIDE...

James is a known e-mail over-checker and over-follow upper. Earlier today, he sent an e-mail to Jacob that has a same-day deliverable. He has an expectation that Jacob will get the e-mail, read it, and reply to him instantaneously. And yet, that rarely happens (and he knows why, that person has a million other priorities like everybody else). So, he grows impatient like a family with young children waiting for a table on a crowded Friday night hoping that they are the next table of five. Jacob's slow response is in direct conflict with James's e-mail stalker persona.

When three hours pass without a response, James leaves his desk and visits Jacob in person. James arrives at Jacob's desk and immediately becomes frustrated, as he has not arrived in the middle of a work-related conversation, but a detailed review of last night's game. James breaks his own rule about not being rude and interrupts a conversation he was not in at the onset. He blurts out: "Jacob, did you get my e-mail?"

CuBe Tips

Stalking at the workplace is never good. However, I realize that missing a deliverable can be at direct odds with your inner stalker tendencies. The key for you is to build relationships and communicate well with your cross-functional work colleagues. When you send an e-mail that is stamped RFN, then they know that you mean business. Just make sure that you do not abuse the privilege or you will lose the faith or your colleagues and become the boy who cried deadline.

Chapter 9

ALL OF THE WONDERS OF THE INTERNET

The World Wide Web can provide so many great things: photos, videos, news articles, data—it can help you solve business problems instantly. But, BEWARE. And be very, very afraid. The allure of immediate answers can lure you into a web of another kind—a trap where time and focus are lost within this black widow's wwweb. Is it really mission critical, right this very second, to see how many likes you got on the photo you posted on Facebook last night?

The Internet, intranets, shared drives, and portals all believe in varying levels of security, too. The problem is that there is not a consistent means of verifying you belong. You cannot simply punch in your name and your own personal password that works everywhere (why not, I ask, why not?). Access can destroy morale as you wait on hold to reset your password because you entered the wrong one eight times and were locked out against your wishes.

Out of Passwords

There is so much data in the world today. Sales reports. TPS reports. P&L statements. And most of these reports are stored on a shared drive (we only share with a few, let's be honest), an intranet, or on the World Wide Web itself. And to get to this cherished data, we are confronted with barriers to entry in the form of usernames and passwords. Let's go INSIDE…

Look at Chris over there. He is visibly frustrated. He just pressed every key on the keyboard at once. He received the requisite beeps in reply from the computer. He cannot access one of the company's data portals—he forgot his username or password or both.

You'd think that one username and password per person would work in the world. One social security number, one username, one password—that's Chris, he's all set. But *no*, every site has its own rules, and Chris needs 107 different combinations to gain access to all of this data.

And these passwords come in all shapes and sizes. Some are numbers. Some are numbers AND letters. And some are CASE SENSITIVE. *Oh*, Chris doesn't want to hurt that poor little sensitive password's feelings.

And just when Chris gets these passwords memorized, he discovers that they are like milk and coupons and they expire. And it's not like the website designers aren't aware of the problem. On most of these sites, it says, "Forgot your username or password?" They know forgetful Chris is coming. Why is this OK?

And do you think they make it easy for Chris to retrieve his password…nope. He finally gives up entering every combination he can think of and gives in by hitting that little link to reset his password.

Instead of simply reminding Chris what he forgot by sending him his password, they send him a 17-character temporary password (q$hyR45Snveta89@j) that he has ZERO chance of remembering. He knows he will be right back in this same situation the next time he comes to this site.

Chris has tried a few times to stay in front of this, but it's an impossible task. He has a ratty sheet of paper crammed in a drawer with usernames and passwords highlighted and crossed out all over the sheet. He is trying to contain the chaos, but he knows he is failing.

And here's another thing about passwords: Chris is out. He's done. He has NONE left. He has already used every living creature that has played the role of pet in his life from childhood to adult, including fish that lived less than 24 hours. He has used his kids' names frontward and backward, the initials of every member of his family, sports stars and their jersey numbers...he is OUT.

CUBE TIPS

We crave data, and we desire simple access. Access is harder than it should be, but we can persevere without requiring a proper execution of the Trojan Rabbit from *Monty Python and the Holy Grail*. So I encourage all of you to create a simple Excel spreadsheet of all of your usernames AND passwords (you must include those pesky, easily forgotten usernames). Then, make sure your admin has a copy of the non-personal entries in this file as well. Hours and hours of stress will be instantly removed. And if you are a manager, you will look like a genius for encouraging your team to compile a similar list.

THE INTERNET DISTRACTION

We all like to be creative. Even if we don't *think* we are creative, we all have special talents and skills. Sometimes at the office, a thought will jump into our heads that is a simple creative addition to a project. Often, that will require further validation or discovery.

And many times, that discovery takes place on the World Wide Web. Let's go INSIDE...

Look, there's Kristin, sitting at her desk working on a PowerPoint presentation. She appears to have had a big idea pop into her head. She needs a picture of a light bulb to make the opening slide spectacular. Big ideas=a light bulb, get it? So, she heads off to the Internet in search of the perfect light bulb picture to deliver her vision. But she quickly veers way off course...

Her home page is Yahoo!. But before she can even enter "light bulb image" into the search box, she is instantly distracted by all that Yahoo! has to offer. Ten minutes later, she has a problem. She now knows the ten most livable cities in America. She can tell you five smart ways to save on gas. She has watched that cute baby video that's all the rage 11 times. But now she has NO IDEA what she is doing on the Internet. So, she starts retracing her keyboard strokes, and then a light bulb goes off in her head...

CuBe TiPs

Yahoo.com cannot be your home page. It simply provides more distractions than a toy store to a five-year-old. Google used to be safe, but now they play with their logo so much that you end up on a chase to figure that out, including a playable Pac Man game. So pick something boring for your work home page. It will save you the trouble and you'll never get lost on the Internet again. Or, even better, set your homepage to your company's website and be a team player.

SOCIAL MEDIA

Social media is a reality of today's business world. Facebook is a place that provides you with an endless array of pictures of your friend's dinner entrees but also an invaluable marketing machine for companies and brands. We live in a 2.0 and 3.0 world, and everyone is communicating in real time. Publicly. For all to see. It's right there instantly on Facebook and Twitter, which can provide massive distractions at work. Let's go INSIDE...

Wes loves to keep his Facebook status up to date. He will "like" all of your posts and is a comment machine. If you are his friend and you have posted something on Facebook, he has seen it. Let's be honest, Wes is addicted to Facebook.

This addiction means Wes must be on Facebook throughout his workday. Wes cannot function without checking out what is going on in the lives of his friends and family. If Wes posts something in the morning, he has in his mind the number of likes and comments he thinks he should get. He watches the polls like a political candidate watches the returns on Election Day. Wes is well aware of the potential negative association that people seeing Facebook on his screen could create. So Wes has perfected a skill. Wes is phenomenal, top five in the country, at jumping to a work-related page when he senses someone is walking near his cube.

Wes is also a frequent Tweeter. He gets all of his sports info here. One hundred and forty characters at a time, Wes is learning something about the world. Wes will often discover something about the business world or his company on Twitter, straight from the customer's mouth.

Cube Tips

The use of Facebook and other social media platforms is a hot debate at companies everywhere. It can absolutely be a drain on productivity if your workplace is filled with a bunch of people like Wes trying to set "like" records for their status updates. I recommend a cautious approach—allow access but let the users know that Facebook should be used for business purposes only (knowing full well that your employees will check it on occasion, much like they make personal calls on their business phones). In moderation, having a Facebook break in the day can be a good refresher before diving back into the day's task at hand.

Twitter is a whole other story. Do you tweet at work? What about your colleagues? If I had said that a few years ago, I probably would have been fired because it has an "adults only" sound to it. Encourage your coworkers to get a Twitter account. And you MUST have one. You don't have to tweet a single time, but be a frequent tweet reader (no one cares if you tweet or not, and one day you might just add your own 140-character view of a topic). Search for your company's name. Search for things you are passionate about. See what's trending in your section of the country, in the US, in the world. This is the best source for instantaneous info about anything. You and your team should NEVER be caught off guard about the news and opinions of your company or industry. #youmustdothis

MEETINGS

You probably spend somewhere between 20% and 50% of your workweek in meetings. Fifty percent! That is insane—some of you might feel like the number is higher (and some weeks it probably is).

You are probably in a constant sprint from one meeting room to another, battling for meeting room space, trying to find time for a quick bathroom break, and wishing for a quick refreshment. Some days feel like the New York City marathon, and you are hoping, nay praying, that they will have one of those drink stations set up and someone will hand you a couple of Dixie cups of water—one to drink in one gulp and the other to splash in your face to keep you focused for the next meeting in the endless series.

The meetings come in three sizes: (1) the small or typical weekly business meeting you have in a smaller meeting room, (2) larger, better attended, more important meetings in larger meeting rooms, and (3) the big national meeting where most members of the company attend at a beautiful third party location, typically a hotel. All are important and throw different types of curveballs at you.

Chapter 10

THE DOUBLE-BOOKED CALENDAR

You know what's really affecting morale? The calendar. People are just shocked and overcome when they stare into their calendars. They cannot believe how full they are—Santa's sack of toys (let alone his rotund belly) is not as full as most people's calendars. Let's go INSIDE…

Look over there…Melissa is staring at her computer screen, specifically her calendar for the day, and she is flabbergasted by her calendar. She can see it. She knows it is there. And yet, it is so unbelievable that she cannot imagine its existence. She cannot believe it got *this* way. And finally, she cannot imagine who let this happen…regardless of the fact that this is indeed just her calendar, not anyone else's. She cannot believe how busy she is. She must be important.

And you know what, other people's calendars are affecting her more than her own. Because by some miracle she cannot fully understand, everyone in the office seems to be suffering from some sort of disease entitled "double booked." Because whenever anyone mentions being double, or the even more severe "triple" booked, they wince as if a shooting pain was running up their back.

The stress this calendar is putting on people is unbelievable. Melissa is now walking over to see if John might have 30 minutes to discuss the Richards project. He pulls up his calendar and then gives her the "there is *NO WAY* that I am going to be able to fit anything in tomorrow," as if his calendar was Kobyashi's mouth and this meeting was hot dog number 59—it's just not gonna fit.

Melissa has colleagues who carry around a printed copy of their calendars, despite owning both a BlackBerry and iPhone (one for work, one for home), so that this double-booked disease can be shown to all that might be in earshot. "Look at this," they say to her, holding up the sheet of paper as proof. "There are three, count 'em, three, rectangles on that line from ten to eleven. I am triple booked."

And every office has two or three senior executives whose calendars are so crazy, or nuts, or whatever adjective you want to use, that they are held almost in awe. Oh, there is NO WAY you can get on Jack's calendar this month. Calendars like Jack's should be held in one of those top-secret, airtight, laser-protected cases like the original Declaration of Independence in DC. This calendar holds a power that will cause Melissa to beg and cajole another human being, usually an amazing admin, for time. You know she lost all logical thought when she said: "Well, would Jack be willing to meet at 5:45 a.m. on this since he appears to be booked until next year?"

Cube Tips

Meetings (and specifically their impact on calendars) are destroying productivity in offices across the country. They allow us to be inefficient with our time. We are always meeting, but we are never working. We are talking and communicating, but we are not getting anything done. I highly recommend

that you take back control of your calendar. Block off at least 90 minutes per day to reserve for you—no meetings, not serving at another person's wishes. This will enable you to stay ahead of your priorities, and you can close the book on those being double booked.

Chapter 11

WEEKLY MEETINGS, WEEKLY CHALLENGES

THE ROOM RESERVATION STARE DOWN AT THE OK CORRAL

Sometimes simple things at the office create some very awkward moments. Something as simple as arriving at a shared meeting room can create a showdown. Let's go INSIDE…

Fred arrives at the meeting room door. It's the top of the hour. No peephole. His posse of three is here. He looks around, peeks over both shoulders, then he forcefully turns the handle and throws that door open. He has this room reserved (or so he thinks). And the folks gathered around the table and the projector and the maze of wires stare back at him, startled like a lightning bolt had just hit. Then, from six paces, there is a stare down between Fred's group and the group in the room.

If this was the OK Corral, it might sound something like this: "Pardner, this here room's mine, and I'm the sheriff in these parts."

"Not so fast, cowboy, this is MY turf." The reality is both parties hurriedly dig through their electronic devices, hoping to get off the first virtual bullet, 'cause nobody's moving until Meeting Room Manager (judge AND jury in these parts) declares a winner of this turf war.

Cube Tips

This tip is simple. Ask your Admin to confirm your meeting rooms for big meetings each week to avoid these awkward stare downs at ten paces. And bookmark meeting room manager in your browser so you can pull the trigger first.

The "Sort-Of" Introduction

At work, we are constantly forging new relationships. Most of those occur inside the company—meeting new people on their first day or working with someone from another department for the first time on a project. These are face-to-face, typical human introductions. Let's go INSIDE to understand what happens when we meet new people on a conference call…

Judy is sitting there in the conference room with five work colleagues. It's the beginning of a conference call with a couple of folks from an agency out of town. At the beginning of the call, there are introductions. Judy has never met either of these agency folks. Never laid eyes on them. Never been in the same room. But, at the end of the introductions, one of the agency peeps says it's "nice to meet you." "Well," Judy thinks to herself, "it might be nice to meet my VOICE, but does this really count as actually meeting?" Others even say "nice to meet you" in an e-mail. Maybe it was nice to meet Judy's font, but that's about it.

CUBE TIPS

Always make an effort to meet people in person. That is how "real" relationships are forged. Shallow relationships are forged via technology. Granted, sometimes that is the only intelligent way to work and that is fine. And if the day comes when you and one of your "conference call pals" are attending the same conference, I offer a warning. I guarantee you will inadvertently act a bit too giddy when you finally meet each other. It's like you are two old friends who have not seen each other for several years. Picture the two people running through an airport to meet up and do that hug-twirl thing that couples do. Ok, I took that one a bit too far, but I did so just so your giddiness doesn't go too far over the top.

OH, THE THINGS WE SAY: GUESS I MISSED THE MEMO

"Oh, the Things We Say" will be sprinkled throughout the book. These are phrases that are easily recognized and often repeated in workplaces everywhere. Let's go INSIDE for this one…

If you go into a meeting, and four of the five people in the meeting are wearing blue shirts, 100 out of 100 times, the person not wearing the blue shirt will say, "Oh, I guess I missed the memo about the blue shirt." No, everyone else independently dressed themselves this morning. There was NOT a memo. Nobody typed or texted anything about wearing blue shirts. Everyone else looked into their sad closets, wished everyone wore a uniform, and settled on blue—which resulted in 80% of the people in the meeting wearing the same uniform.

The Smart Phone Is Making Us Look Dumb

Technology is constantly changing. And it enables us to be more connected to the office, information, and our coworkers than ever before. But is this a good thing? Let's go INSIDE…

Erica loves her iPhone. It is smaller than the triangular-shaped Super Phone, but even more powerful. Erica simply cannot survive without it. When she doesn't have it, she cannot function. If she is without her phone for an extended period of time, she would literally melt into the carpeting like the Wicked Witch of the West.

This device was originally designed for when Erica was OUT of the office…but she is getting a ton of use IN the office. And this creates some childlike behavior. Because of her addiction, she cannot help herself. She has to be up to date on everything, all the time, right now, live.

So, Erica will sit there in a meeting, completely ignoring the presenter…then she looks around to see if the coast is clear and sneaks that iPhone out of its little holster on her belt. Then she puts up the impenetrable hand shield, and starts rolling through messages that came up during the meeting.

Memo to Erica: WE CAN SEE YOU! WE CAN SEE YOU! It's just like the kid that sucked at hide and seek…we can see you.

CuBe TiPs

Stop the madness. Smart phone use in meetings should be kept to an absolute minimum. It is rude, outrageous, and quite frankly, unproductive, because most of these in-meeting e-mail readers only get 50% of the facts from their sneaky, half-read e-mail on the iPhone and have to go back to their desk to read the entire thing.

THE SORCERER OF TIME

Sitting next to you in your cube, or on another floor, there are sorcerers. People with the special, magical ability to grant you time. Let's go INSIDE…

Joe is one of those people that love to make lists during the day and cross things off when he completes a task. And if he is in a meeting with an agenda, you better believe he will be checking off each agenda item.

Today is no different, and Joe is tracking through the agenda of an hour-long meeting. About 30 minutes into it, he realizes he has checked off all of the agenda items. So then Roger, the leader of the meeting (and the self-appointed sorcerer of time) gets out his magic time wand and says, "Well, that about wraps up everything for today, so I am going to *give* you thirty minutes back into your day."

Where exactly are these 30 minutes located? Does today have 24 and one half hours in it? Of course not. Roger just poorly scheduled his meeting.

CuBe TiPs

Everyone's calendar is "a mess" or "crazy." So, properly scheduling your meeting is a challenge—can you get the right people, for the proper amount of time?

Do NOT have a senior level meeting when only two of the three key decision makers can attend or you will DEFINITELY be having that meeting twice. Find a time when all can attend and get closure on your business topic.

As it relates to the length of the meeting, try your best to be concise and deliver what you need in 30 minutes. Sometimes, a topic has the potential for 45–60 minutes, so do plan accordingly. Nothing is worse than rushing an important topic or having the next group show up for the room and you are not anywhere near finished. So, try to be respectful of the schedules of others. But here's one thing about getting done early: even if you could have and should have scheduled 30 minutes instead of 60, we're buying into the whole sorcerer of time thing. "We got 30 minutes back, BABY! WOOHOO!

Travel Time Is Not Included

Do you know how hard it is to be on time? I have always been a stickler for timely arrival at meetings and events at the office. Yet, the very set-up makes it nearly impossible. Let's go INSIDE…

Jerry's schedule is loaded with back-to-back meetings. He is sprinting from one to the next, and he is facing a perilous situation: he's either going to be late or his bladder will explode. Or, he faces a five-minute walk from one corner of the building to another and he's gonna be late. Period.

CuBe Tips

Please, for the love of all that is right in this world, choose being late over "holding it" like a toddler in the backseat of a road trip who suddenly has to go right now and it's 11 miles to the next rest area. Please take care of business, "pay the water bill," or "take a bio break" (all right enough already; this is getting gross).

For the meetings you lead and attend, try to encourage things to wrap up five minutes early. You will help your colleagues in more ways than just being on time for their next meeting.

Chapter 12

BIG MEETINGS, BIG AUDIENCES, BIG ISSUES

POWERPOINT PITFALLS

There are many pitfalls when creating a PowerPoint deck to be presented in a large group session. First, you need to get the information just right. If you accomplish that, you should be golden. But the way you prepare and present the slides can make or break the information on the slides. Let's go INSIDE...

Rachel is a Microsoft Office wizard. She knows every macro and every short cut in Excel. When she is reviewing budgets, her fingers move faster than a master pianist in the middle of "Flight of the Bumblebees." Numbers become charts in seconds. Elaborate pivot tables are a piece of cake.

The same holds true for PowerPoint. When she creates her presentations, she must think she is competing for *Guinness Book of World Records* for the most builds, clicks, and animations on one PowerPoint slide. She thinks it is really cool when one pie chart explodes and changes color.

Rachel loves presenting her Excel data in PowerPoint. She will cram 45 rows of numbers on one slide because she can. When she presents this page, she states the halfway apologetic, halfway uncomfortable: "Sorry about the eye chart, but…"

CuBe Tips

Tell a simple story. Sure, you can add some builds, but only if they BUILD your story. This isn't elementary school where the kid with the best binder will get the best grade. I want a deck that leads me to the solution of a business problem. And I want that answer as succinctly and quickly as possible.

When presenting, don't offer eye charts. If you know it is an eye chart, donate it to your local optometrist to replace the one with the big E at the top. And if you really are the only thing between the audience and lunch, don't remind them of that or they will be focused on their individual strategies to secure a chocolate chip cookie.

If you do have mad PowerPoint skills, put them to use at home. Wow Grandma Ruth and Uncle Billy with the most amazing vacation slide show they've ever seen with dissolves, music, etc. Just keep those to a minimum at the workplace.

Function F4getaboutit

Sometimes you just want technology to work. It can mean the difference between having a great day at work and a bad one. It can be the turning point in your career if a key presentation is derailed by a PowerPoint without power. Let's go INSIDE…

John brought his laptop to the big meeting room. The crowd of 50+ has gathered. He's hooked up the cable. And the screen doesn't show his beautiful PowerPoint cover slide. It shows a blue image with white type that says "No Image," or "Searching for Image," or the rather sassy, "Do you want me to display an image, or what?" OK, that last one might be made up.

Then three or four so-called computer experts in the meeting yell, "Function F4, function F4" like they just figured out a drawing in a game of Pictionary. John has hit Function F4 71 times and it still hasn't changed. So now there's the scramble to find the cell number of the company AV guy. What a train wreck…pure chaos on display for everyone sitting in the uncomfortable, big meeting chairs that are way too close together and don't have an armrest.

CuBe TiPs

If you are making a big presentation in one of those BIG, important conference rooms, block the 30 minutes prior to your meeting and preset everything so you are ready. Test the AV so our ears are not blasted by the music. Please make sure the speakers don't buzz and hiss for the 57 minutes when your three-minute video isn't playing (that can be a bigger distraction than any typo on a slide). And kindly move the arrow from the middle of your video when we're watching it. Skooch the arrow to the side; it distracts us.

The Smart Phone Walkie-Talkie

Sometimes you want to communicate across a large meeting room with a colleague. Most of the time, you want to text something funny about what was said, what was on the screen, you know, very juvenile, high school stuff that can add a little levity to a long meeting. But sometimes, you need to get important information that pertains to the presentation. You need to communicate NOW. You need walkie-talkies. If this was like the "Seer Gilligan" episode of *Gilligan's Island*, then we could read each other's minds. But that's not feasible. So let's go INSIDE and watch that scene unfold...

Eric is in a large and important meeting. He is the next presenter. His boss, Allison, is across the room. Eric is reviewing his talking points for the discussion. His phone is on mute. And Allison is dying to get a hold of him. She has to tell him not to present the financials, as she just got new information. But does Eric look up? No.

She is literally staring a hole through him without him having any idea. Eric will be blindsided if she can't get a hold of him, and he is on in five minutes. She decides to create a distraction and loudly bumps the table as she rearranges her chair. Eric looks up. Allison holds up her phone and points to it—the universal symbol of "I realize I am pointing at MY phone, but you need to look at YOUR phone right now." Crisis averted.

CuBe TiPs

Establish a protocol with your team in big meetings that enables you to help each other via text—but only if necessary. TEXTING DURING A MEETING IS 98% RUDE. But, if real-time information is needed, or clarification will help with a presentation, make sure you have an easy way to communicate (until we develop the food or serum that enables us to read each other's minds—and then every meeting will be complete chaos).

THE BLANK PIECE OF PAPER

Perception is reality as people walk around the halls of an office. What people wear, when people arrive and depart, and even how they take notes is being scrutinized (or so most people think). Let's go INSIDE...

Sonia is heading to the company-wide meeting held by the senior executives. This is a high-level meeting that Sonia has been to many times in the past. She has never taken a single note at one of these meetings. Yet, what does she make sure she does before leaving her desk for the meeting? She grabs a pen and a notepad and heads to the meeting. And as she looks around the room, nearly every lap is holding a writing utensil and some form of parchment—all to be left blank at the end of the session.

CuBe TiPs

If it's convenient to head by your desk on the way to the meeting, grab a pen and pad; it's not going to hurt you. But don't risk being late by going back to your desk for that sole purpose—the Bic people are not selling pens based on this meeting.

Chapter 13

NATIONAL SALES MEETING

Many companies have a national sales meeting. It's the marquee event each year. A large conference hotel is chosen. Each morning, a large chunk of the company's employees gather to nibble on tasty hotel vittles in large hotel ballrooms. Conference rooms come to life with sizzling presentations designed to inspire one and all.

Beware the pressures of this meeting. There are pre-reads. There are breakout sessions. There are never-ending "happy hours." An event designed to boost morale for the group can actually drag your individual morale down due to the choices you make throughout the day (and night).

Hotel Fun Camp

When you check into a hotel on a business trip, it's like you are checking into Hotel Fun Camp. Let's go INSIDE…

Patrick can never seem to get his keycard to work on the first try when attempting to enter his hotel room. But once he passes through that door, he loses his mind. His behavior is irrational, as if he has been brainwashed to behave like a ten-year-old.

As Patrick finishes a bag of cheese curls, do you think he reaches for a napkin or paper towel? Nope, full-sized bath towels to get that orange residue off of his fingers. And when he is done with the towel, he whips it into the corner of the room—it's Hotel Fun Camp; he doesn't seem to have a care in the world.

Since he arrived late and missed dinner, he orders room service. At the end of his phone call for his order of a chicken sandwich, fries, and a soft drink, the staff member says, "Thirty-three sixteen." That is not his room number, but the price. Hotel Fun Camp is truly crazy.

His food arrives, and he scarfs down his pricey meal. Then it is time for the perfectly acceptable, though simply audacious, next step in this eating process. Patrick decides to do the dishes. He throws all of the remnants of his meal on the tray, marches those unsightly remains to the door, opens the door, and sets that tray in the hallway for everyone to see. And this is perfectly acceptable behavior.

It is now after 10:30 at night and the pre-read materials on Patrick's bed are quickly becoming the "didn't read" materials, because Patrick makes a classic Hotel Fun Camp mistake—he turns on the TV. Whenever you turn on a TV after 10:00 p.m. in a hotel, your brain is simply unable to discern the difference between a good and bad television program or movie. Patrick spends the next two hours watching *Police Academy 6* because that Michael Winslow is one funny cat. It's 1:45 in the morning before Patrick shuts down Hotel Fun Camp for the night.

Cube Tips

When you are travelling on business, it is easy to get distracted. Your coworkers will be one definite distraction, but the hotel itself is another. When you have a big meeting in the morning, do NOT turn on the TV. Go to bed, get a good night's sleep. There are

simply too many bad shows that look way too good once you have been brainwashed by the mysterious Hotel Fun Camp.

THE WALK-IN BUDDY SYSTEM

When you travel to a national corporate meeting, there are so many things that affect your performance that have nothing to do with the content of the meeting. Your hair, your clothes, and even the people you walk into the meeting rooms with are being scrutinized. You need a walk-in buddy. Let's go INSIDE…

John is heading down to the lobby for the start of the big national sales meeting, but he needed to do some pre-planning, and he regrets it. He did not set up a meeting location with his people. When he walks into the general assembly, he must have a walk-in buddy. Right now, he doesn't know where his people are—and he is in a panic to find them.

So, as John is looking for his people, a woman walks toward him, who he kind of recognizes from the prior year's meeting. And she says, "Hey, John."

"*GREAT,* first names are in play," thinks John.

John is racking his brain to remember his name, but nothing is coming to him. And, unfortunately for John, the type on the name badges is so small that he cannot make out her name (nor does he wish to be caught staring where her name badge is currently lodged).

John's listening skills are poor because he is multi-tasking: he is trying to spot a walk-in buddy and remember this woman's name all at the same time. He is failing in both areas.

When, suddenly, this woman approaches, it's her "walk-in buddy" and she says, "Hey, Cynthia, you ready to find a seat?" So, John says, "Great seeing you, Cynthia," like he had it all along.

But here's the problem with John's Cynthia project…it took time away from finding a walk-in buddy. And then they start with the lightning or the mood music...isn't there an easier way to let us know that the meeting is about to start than to have the staff flick the lights on and off at a thousand miles an hour or have a guy wearing gloves stroll through the lobby with his oversized xylophone? And John is out of luck.

He needs his entourage. He needs his Turtle, Drama, and Eric. This is the way he shows the rest of the company how he rolls and he has nobody. He knows if he is forced to walk into the "G-A" by himself, they might as well reprint his name badge: L-O-S-E-R.

So, he is panicked, when all of a sudden he spots Kevin from Procurement. He doesn't really know him that well, so he strikes up a sports conversation and says, "Let's go grab some seats."

And, as they walk into the meeting room, for the fourth consecutive year, "Let's Get It Started" by the Black Eyed Peas is blaring out of the speakers.

CuBe TiPs

Perception is a big part of morale. Yes, many people are panicked about who will sit next to them in the uncomfortable hotel meeting room chairs. So, remember to preset a meeting place with your walk-in buddies and this stress will walk away.

THE GENERAL ASSEMBLY BLUES

When there is a large gathering of employees, with a stage, a podium, and a CEO reading off a teleprompter, you are distracted by the material in the presentations by four specific things: (1) successfully turning off your cell phones; (2) staying awake; (3) timing your return during breaks; and (4) avoiding interaction with the presenter at all costs. Let's go INSIDE...

The GA, or general assembly, is about to begin. *BHT: at every national sales meeting or big company event I ever attended, it always starts with "housekeeping issues" to cover. I always checked my holster: no Dustbuster and no Swiffer. How did this particular phrase get started? I left my supplies at home, pal, so you are dusting solo.

Lauren is sitting in the audience, with her walk-in buddies.

The emcee asks the audience to silence their phones. Lauren looks around, and more than half the audience is digging in their pants and purses to check their phones. Then the CEO is introduced. *BHT: I love the fact that he feels compelled to run up on stage when he's introduced. "Yes sir, I am in great shape! I ran up three steps! You have one fit CEO."

Lauren's biggest fear is that her cell phone, which she turned off 10 minutes ago, will magically turn itself on and ring. She does not want to be THAT person. Then it happened. Right there in the GA. And remember, phones don't ring, they play music. And in this particular incident, the phone is playing the Go-Go's "We've Got the Beat" REALLY, REALLY loud.

The CEO at the podium is playing through it, "Our sales have reached new heights this year as we keep...going up, up, up, like a ba-loon..."

So Lauren looks over to see how this poor woman is going to handle this phone situation. Oh my lord, it's a GUY. She hopes he lost a bet, seriously...the Go Gos? So, he's fumbling around trying not to make a bad situation worse, because it can be rough to get something out of your front pants pocket. He finally gets it loose and when that phone hits the fresh air, it is REALLY loud...it's like Belinda Carlisle is actually in the room, singing her heart out. He finally gets it turned off. And all of the folks sitting around him have that look on their faces—that really strict librarian look, "I'm really disappointed in you."

So, it's one suit after another. They run up on stage, they do their speech, they thank us, and off they go. It's been over 90 minutes, and Lauren has turned into that toddler from the car again, crossing and uncrossing her legs. She is saved by the emcee who says, "We're on a tight schedule, but we are going to take a quick ten-minute bio break (there it is again)."

*BHT: The other thing that's interesting to me is that no meeting in the history of corporate America has ever restarted at the time requested by the emcee. He always looks at his watch and begs me, but it never works. Why is that? There are never any repercussions. The group philosophy is this: you guys can go ahead and present to the chairs if you like, but we are all going to be out here in the lobby for several more minutes. I do have a suggestion that would solve this problem. They simply need to say, "We will cancel this afternoon's fresh-baked chocolate chip cookies if everybody is not back in ten minutes." I know every seat would be filled after nine minutes and 33 seconds.

So, then they bring the CEO back up for Q&A, where he takes questions from the audience. Now, some people want to get their issues out, and you know what Lauren says to them…go for it. She is in full turtle mode. She will bend down and act like she is tying both shoes (and she is wearing heels). She knows she cannot, at any cost, make eye contact with him. She does not want to have to produce a question under this duress. *BHT: if FBI agents were smart, they'd give up the small rooms and bright lights and scare tactics to get a criminal to talk. They should simply put the accused in a national sales meeting GA and have the CEO call his name.

As Lauren looks around the audience of people who are not wearing footwear with shoestrings, 300 people have all immediately decided that their laces seem a little loose.

CuBe TiPs

Review what buttons could accidentally be bumped that turn your ringer from off to Go-Gos. And for a complete disaster check, plan a good question or two. Meeting planners: please help these people out—they feel like accused criminals during the CEO's Q&A. Help them embrace the chance to have their voice be heard in a setting like this (a good question can enhance one's standing within the organization...as can a bad one in a negative fashion).

The Break Outs

While the high-level general assembly presentations are a critical portion of any company agenda, the details are found in the breakouts. But, there's a problem. You treat the breakouts like you treated a second-semester, senior-year high school history class. Let's go INSIDE…

Brandon survived the GA, and then it's time for the breakouts. But Brandon has no idea where the breakout rooms are. In fact, nobody seems to have a clue. Three hundred people are pouring out of the GA room and heading exactly nowhere in particular. *BHT: Why are all hotel meeting rooms named after trees and presidents? The budget breakout is in Van Buren 4. The planning breakout is in Maple 2.

The breakouts are as close as Brandon gets to high school, because he sits in the back with his friends. He blatantly passes notes back and forth to people sitting at the table in front of his. He knows he is not being the best audience member, but after the GA, he can't seem to contain himself.

*BHT: The person I love to watch in the breakouts is the scribe in the front of the room at the flip chart. These people see this as a chance to show off their creativity. At my last meeting, I distinctly remember one of these Leonardo da Sharpie types. He wrote the first letter M in blue, then recapped, then the next letter A in purple, and recapped, then the R in yellow, which no one could see; it was actually a misplaced highlighter, and recapped. It took him eight minutes to write the word "Marketing," and it was all going downhill at a 45-degree angle...no one can write very well on a flip chart, either.

Suddenly, the presenter asks for a volunteer, and one of Brandon's walk-in buddies "volunteers" him. Brandon is being asked to scribe the balance of the meeting on the flip chart. The bad news for Brandon is that he doesn't spell very well.

The brainstorming session starts and Brandon is doing well, smiling and having fun. Then someone yells out "hieroglyphics." Brandon's face was immediately shrouded in panic. He got the H...he got the H. But then there was a "Y" up there and at one point, five consonants in a row, so he got fed up, crossed out the entire multi-colored word with the black marker, and wrote the word "symbols" and headed back to his chair, frustrated.

CuBe TIPs

Be aware of the impact you will have on both sides of the breakout. If you are presenting, you need to be confident, well rehearsed, and ready to overcome a room full of distractions. If you or someone you know struggles in the area of spelling or penmanship, step in and save the day.

If you are one of the "jokers" in the back of the room, a little fun is fine, but do not create a distraction. Support your colleagues, and try not to yell out words like "connoisseur" that are tough to spell during brainstorm sessions.

THE TRAINING SESSION

You want to get better and improve your skills. You want to find ways to do things better, faster, and smarter. You want to work on areas that need personal development. You will embrace these opportunities. Yet, it is the WAY that you are trained that requires a dive INSIDE...

Jessica sits at the front of the typical training room. The instructor is fiddling with the flip chart and data projector. He then taps on the table and is ready to conduct his orchestra (Jessica and her classmates) with a "Fine Point Bullet Tip White Board Marker."

He tells a quick, humorous, animated story about a fishing trip he took three years ago and shares intricate details about a three-hour battle of wills with a gigantic blue marlin. He's had weeks, years even, to prepare his intro. Jessica may get 10 seconds because now he wants a member of the class to share a few tidbits.

Jessica is sitting there, looking at her fellow trainees around the horseshoe-shaped table, fidgeting like kindergartners on the first day of school. Everyone is doing everything in his or her power to avoid eye contact with the trainer. The question everyone wants answered is simple: How is this guy going to pick the person who goes first with the introductions?

Jessica does not want to be the person that goes first. She knows that requires being funny—RIGHT NOW. She came to this class to be trained, not to perform and get laughs. What if she tells what she thinks is a funny story and all she hears are crickets? She knows she will get ZERO out of the training session because of the crickets.

Jessica exhales, as she is NOT the first person to go, but she is quickly dreaming up something to say. In her mind she hopes that the "performance" of the person going before her is merely average (she doesn't want failure, but she sure doesn't want someone to "kill it" either).

The other thing that distracts Jessica is the agenda. She enjoys following along with the incredibly specific times that are associated with each topic. She is especially concerned with the timing of critical agenda items with one-word titles like "Break" or "Lunch." If it looks like a topic is running long that leads up to breaks or lunch, Jessica and her peers suddenly have the attention span of a seven-year-old at Toys 'R' Us.

The agenda page also serves as her special canvas—it gives her the chance to color. Throughout the day, when things drag a bit, she will color in the Os on the agenda. And if she gets desperate for something to do, she'll even fill in that little top part of the lower case "e."

Jessica does enjoy watching the instructor conduct the class and wield that marker—when he wants to really make a point, he will double or triple underline a word. Or, better yet, he completes two underlines with one color, then transfers to another color for two more. But, if this point is so critical that the world as we know it may end if the class does not learn it, the conductor pulls out his final, most expressive move. He circles the word, not once, not twice, but 300 times, so that the class cannot even see the word now and he has ripped through three layers of flip chart paper.

Jessica does enjoy going to training classes and is there to seek knowledge, but if the class can end a little early, there will be zero complaints from her. If it's looking like the class is ahead on the agenda, she will shut it down. The instructor will ask, "Any questions?"

Jessica shakes her head violently back and forth like a pitcher shaking off a sign from the catcher. Then she leads her colleagues as they all stare down the chatty person who loves to hear himself talk, mouthing the words "don't you dare."

This particular class has had that guy, Todd, who wouldn't stop talking about issues that only pertained to him. The entire class is now focused on him, wishing lasers would come out of all of their eyes so he is unable to speak up.

All training classes end in the same manner, with an evaluation form, name optional. The jokesters sign it "Fred Flintstone," the paranoid leave it blank, and the go getters sign it with their real name so they get credit (you better believe I was there).

Jessica fills out every evaluation form the same way. On a five-point scale, she circles four for the first item, then four for the next question, then four, then four again, and just so every one of them isn't a four, she gives the last one a three or a five, depending on how good the class was.

CuBe TiPs

You must focus on the benefits of the class, not the way it is taught (a more engaging trainer will certainly help you avoid these distractions). If you know you get uncomfortable speaking to a larger group or talking about yourself, rehearse a personal intro to help you avoid a "cricket incident."

If you are a manager, schedule a de-brief shortly after the class with the rest of your team so that (1) those who did not attend can gain the applicable knowledge and (2) so those in attendance can gain additional assistance in applying what was learned.

Finally, do your training class attending employees a favor. Tell them that if the class ends early, to head on home, don't worry about trying to make that dreaded decision that comes up when a class ends at 3:30. Even if a few members of the group head back to the office, the rest will enjoy the extra hour at home and appreciate and retain the information from the class they just attended even more.

THE BOSS

Picture your best boss...go ahead, close your eyes and picture this person. They had your back, didn't they? They made coaching you a priority, didn't they? They did the little things that made you feel important. They were there for you when the shitake mushrooms hit the fan. They trusted you, didn't they?

More people leave their jobs because of their boss than because of how much they are paid. A bad boss is often the number one reason people are frustrated in their jobs.

Manage, coach, communicate clearly and a boost in morale will follow closely behind.

Chapter 14

SUNDAY NIGHT & MONDAY MORNING STRESS

Sunday Night Is NOT All Right

My managing friends, the workweek actually starts on Sunday night. This is when your employees' brains switch from weekend mode to work mode to, more specifically, dread mode. Yes, dread…that's just not right. Let's go INSIDE…

It's Sunday night and Jack is sitting on his couch, trying to concentrate on his favorite TV drama, but he can't because the mountain of thoughts about the things he has to do tomorrow at work starts piling up. His air of foreboding cannot be ignored.

Jack knows he tends to obsess and stress about work. His brain is now overwhelmed by the back-to-back meetings that are on his calendar tomorrow. Unfortunately for Jack, these meetings start impacting his life 24 hours early.

So, Jack then feels compelled to tell his spouse that tomorrow is going to be a really long day. "I have to do this; I have to get this done; I have to meet with these people to work on a critical project.

Jack's wife tries to be supportive but doesn't understand the technical aspects of his job. She stares at Jack the same way the dog looks at him when he speak a paragraph to it and the only word that Chubby the Bulldog really understood was "Chubby."

CuBe TiPs

Sunday nights need to be rescued. The dread must be eliminated, or at least minimized. If you are a manager, you can do it. Eliminate early morning meetings on Mondays. Do everything in your power to encourage weekend discussion time. While on the surface this appears to be an anti-productive move, it is actually a big time saver and can rescue your entire team from pop-ins from the notoriously long-winded weekend storyteller. NOTE: the storyteller in the parking lot makes the rounds in the hallways on Monday morning, too.

THE IMPACT OF ROAD RAGE

Managers, many of your employees take deep breaths as they put the key in the ignition and head to work. Many of you may believe the drive to work is a simple task that has NOTHING to do with your team's ability to perform at a high level that day in their jobs. Nothing could be farther from the truth. This is not merely about getting from point A (home) to point B (work). This is Sunday dread on overdrive. Let's go INSIDE…

Terry wishes he could drive to work in a more relaxed state of mind, but he can't, especially on Monday mornings. The traffic, plus the mental checklist of "to dos" and "to don'ts" just starts piling up on him. While he should be playing air guitar when "Pour Some Sugar on Me" comes on the radio, he actually has visions of the office "Pouring Some Serious Work on Him." And he knows the biggest potential challenge of all can occur after he parks and gets out of the car.

C_uB_e T_iP_s

I'm begging you; get your teams off to a good start on Monday mornings. Surprise them with bagels, or donuts, or a muffin, or even a cheesy "have a great day" post-it note on their computer screen. You CAN reset the mindset, but you have to reset yours, too. Don't take these issues for granted. And get good donuts, no pink ones.

Chapter 15

THE ARRIVAL PLAN THAT AVOIDS THE BOSS

There are times your employees want to see you and times that they most definitely do NOT. How sad is that? They should not fear the sight of you….but they do. If they get in a little late, no matter the reason, they are avoiding you like the plague. If they leave just a tad early, they will avoid you like a ninth grader who spots their mom on the opposite side of the mall. In fact, your employees are devising exit strategies…yes, investing time in finding ways to escape from their workplace. Let's go INSIDE…

As Kristin is about to leave the office at the end of the workday, she first has to take a survey of the area. Does it SEEM like there are a lot of people around right now? She doesn't really want to be first to leave, to be the sacrificial lamb…like that poor youngster in most of those medieval movies.

*BHT: You know this kid, the one who is arguing with the leader. He wants to be a man and go to war. Placed at the back of the large warrior grouping and in a safe place, he pushes forward, charging to the front of the line to be the first to engage in combat. And, of course, the first two arrows from the enemy pierce his tiny little

Wal-Mart knight Halloween costume shield and he falls to the turf. Which, of course, INFURIATES the army warrior leader. He runs forward into the mix. Two thousand arrows are flying within inches all around him, but magically just missing, and he single-handedly defeats 1,240 enemy warriors in the next three minutes.

Moral of this story: she can't be brash and take those arrows by leaving too early. She has to review all of the options. So, she has devised three great exit strategies: the sneak out, the fake out, and the stake out.

The first option is the sneak out when she carries nothing. She packs her gear into the drawers in her desk. She shuts down her computer and walks away. As far as everyone knows, she's on her way to a meeting. Or, she can upgrade herself to the super sneak out in which she carries a notepad or blank folder, because she must be heading somewhere important, maybe to a meeting.

In this scenario, she knows she cannot, under any circumstances, say good night to anyone or anybody. She must sell it. She's very busy, and on her way to a very important meeting.

Or she can try the fake out in which she leaves her computer ON, with her e-mail program open, and she sets her screen saver at two hours. Anyone who swings by her desk will KNOW that she MUST be here somewhere.

If Kristin knows that she will be seen, and she is desperate to leave RIGHT NOW, then she can try the "over carry." She will load up her hands with folders that she hasn't looked at for weeks, her computer bag, and at least one box of any size to add to the effect.

She knows if she employs this strategy, she must do the exact opposite of the sneak out. She WANTS to be seen. "Look at me; I have so much work to do tonight that I may pull an all-nighter." She will take the slow, circuitous route and be seen. With all of this stuff, she is clearly a hard worker who is not against taking a large amount of work home.

The easiest option, with the most benefit and very minimal risk, is the stake out. If she has ABSOLUTELY nothing else to do now, but she doesn't want to take one of the aforementioned arrows by going first, it's time to use the Internet to her advantage. She can spend the next hour catching up on her personal e-mail or see the latest on Facebook, but she knows she absolutely cannot leave now. Facebook never had a bigger impact if Kristin leaves one hour later than she had originally planned and she bumps into the VP on her way out

CuBe TiPs

If you are a manager, recognize that your employees might very well be carrying around books, computers, and papers that they do not need because of you. You can stop the charade. Simply tell the members of your team to get their work done on time—that the when and where is irrelevant (within certain guidelines obviously).

If you do not manage people, but manage to have these arrival and departure fears, talk to your boss. Instead of dreaming up creative solutions, simply have a conversation. Then you can walk out with whatever items you really need and not a project binder from ten years ago that is just for show.

Chapter 16

THE POWER OF THE BOSS'S INVOLVEMENT

THE SENIOR LEADER PROJECT FREAK OUT

Projects for senior managers create stress, that's a given. But how you, as a manager, help your team deal with that stress can easily separate those who are successful and those who are not. Let's go INSIDE…

Bruce always adds extra stress to his work with his attachment paranoia. He gets this phobia whenever a senior executive has asked him to prepare some data in a PowerPoint slide or two. He gets worked up about the spacing, and the graphs have to line up perfectly on the page. And he has to save the document and open it 12 times to make sure it saved the last version. His paranoia, believe it or not, escalates from there.

After Bruce types the body of his e-mail to the senior leader (which he has to re-read 41 times), it's time for him to attach the document he worked so diligently to perfect. Only he cannot simply hit the paperclip icon, find the file, hit attach, and hit send. He hits the paperclip, and then he feels compelled to OPEN the attachment as if the document somehow miraculously changed itself *on its own* since he last saved it.

CuBe TiPs

Managers, do not foster an environment of stress. If you tell your team that this is the "most important presentation in the history of the company" (no chance, by the way), then your team will have attachment paranoia to the ninth power. Encourage your team to trust themselves. They know the details of their document way better than the senior leader who's receiving it. Sure, the executive might have questions, but their intent is not to turn you into a second guesser that rivals rabid NFL football fans who wonder why their coach didn't go for it on fourth and one.

If you get attachment paranoia, that shows that you care, which is excellent. But you cannot let that paranoia consume you. Have faith in yourself that the project is complete, and then send it on its way with confidence.

The Positive Pop-In

Most people know how to get their daily work done. Some are certainly more organized than others, but they typically know what they plan to get accomplished on a given day or during a given week. That's assuming a fire drill is not created from above. Sometimes, those cannot be avoided. Let's go INSIDE…

Carrie believes that the only time her boss's boss (or someone higher up the rectangle food chain of an org chart) will visit is when they need something. Directors, and especially vice presidents, never stop by just to check in or praise. She associates their names with tight deadlines and stressful work that will put her behind on the other work she planned to complete on that day.

If Carrie fields a call, e-mail, or text from one of the senior leaders, she believes a crisis, additional work, and problems are coming her way. She dreads opening e-mails from the boss's boss. She gets caller ID paranoia when a senior leader's name pops up on her phone.

Cube Tips

Moral of this story: all managers reading this must be aware of this debilitating trait. You must mix in some no-reason pop-ins to talk sports or family. Even better would be some "atta boy" moments that are sincere and unscripted. Show that you care about the person, not just their work—that is a critical distinction. Flip the perception, and the paranoia of your name will vanish.

The Squeaky Wheel Gets All of the Attention

Every office has those two or three people that will not stop bugging you. Ever. As a manager, you MUST help your team, as these "squeaky wheels" are killing your team's productivity. Let's go INSIDE…

Mark just won't leave Misty alone. He just hangs out near her cube waiting for her. His project is not one of Misty's critical assignments. Yet he's there, three or four times a day. He's wearing out the carpet outside her cube because he'll stay and pace in front of her cube even if she is on the phone.

She can't hide under her desk. Mark even starts bugging her coworkers on her cube street who have nothing to do with the work (and they give HER evil stares when he shows up).

CuBe TiPs

Managers, you MUST step in. Your team cannot have this productivity drain in their day. Talk to the stalker or even the stalker's boss (if necessary) to establish other means to get the job done. Suggest alternative means to improve the flow of information. And make sure you do not aid and abet stalking behavior. Don't jump into the conversation that is clearly a drain on your team member's morale. And for the love of all that is right in the world, do NOT become a cube stalker yourself, under any circumstances.

Chapter 17

THE CORPORATE OFFSITE

THE BOWLING OUTING

Companies are always trying to build camaraderie with their teams. They want you to have fun with your colleagues outside of the office. A common locale for this type of activity is bowling. The whole group heads over to the creatively named Strike Zone, Alley Gators, Bowl Winkles, or Spare Time Lanes. Let's go INSIDE...

As Kenny enters Spare Time Lanes, he is hoping for a good team. At this outing, he is certainly interested in competing, and potentially winning, but his number one priority is having a good time. And that requires having a least one member of his inner work posse on his team. Today, that wish is not granted. Kenny is on a team with coworkers who he does not spend a lot of time with outside of actual work projects. (And isn't that the whole idea of a bowling offsite?)

One member of Kenny's team, Dan, lives for this day. Dan has his own bowling shoes, his own monogrammed ball, a glove, and of course a bowling shirt with his league team name "The Banana Splits." His equipment oozes passion about bowling.

When Dan holds his hand over that little air vent at the end of the ball return, it looks cool. He throws the ball with spin—it looks like it is headed right into the gutter but then the ball spins violently toward the head pin and the rest of the pins explode.

Dan is clearly a great bowler, and Kenny is now very happy to be on his team. Dan loves him some bowling more than most. Kenny was ready to tease everyone who showed up with their own bowling equipment—but when Dan is throwing strike after strike, Kenny secretly wishes he could bowl a game over 225, too.

CuBe TiPs

Every company wants great morale. They want you to be happy and inspired at work. They want a great culture. And they hold outings and offsite activities to encourage the peeps to get to know each other better in a non-work activity.

There is one huge key to these types of outings for the organizers and one for the attendees. For the organizers, any "fun" activity, whether it is bowling or not, must be well organized, easy to keep score (folks like to compete), with ample supplies of food and drink. Mix up the teams—all Kennys should meet all of the Dans.

For attendees like yourself, you must go with the proper attitude. If you are not happy because you got on what you think is the "bad" team, then take responsibility and make it the "good" or "great" team. You are bowling for work—that sounds pretty great right off the top—have fun and make some stronger connections with your coworkers.

THE GOING-AWAY PARTY

People leave companies for lots of different reasons. Some are moving because their spouse got a new job. Some found a great new job that perfectly fits their talents (or pays them way more money or gives them better career advancement). Some are becoming stay-at-home moms and dads. Some are going to be entrepreneurs and start their own business. But no matter the reason, they are leaving. And if they have been with the company for at least three years, there needs to be a going-away party. Let's go INSIDE…

Look at this scene over here at the local pub that's just a couple of miles from the office. One after another, people are rolling into the office to celebrate Leslie, who is leaving the company after five years. As people arrive, they are greeted by a caricature of Leslie (that says "Thanks for the Memories") and a Sharpie.

This event has now become the last day of school. As each person arrives, they must suddenly be creative. And most are clearly not ready. A few just want the beer on the company's tab and sign it with a simple "Good luck" and a signature. The resident creative and class clown signs it HAGS, Ryan. *BHT: HAGS = Have a Great Summer.

Others, who are there so that senior leaders see them (yes, they are going to a party for someone who is leaving because they are certain this will help their future advancement to show that they are a supportive teammate even though the last time they talked to Leslie was three months ago), take a few minutes and try to write something that will look impressive when others read it.

There is much milling about. The people that usually talk to each other and go to lunch with each other are talking to each other now. Leslie is clearly the star of the show. And Leslie is the only person in this group who will NOT be working for the company next week (that we know of).

There is a lot of attention paid to the attendance of senior leaders of the department. There is a direct correlation, in the eyes of the attendees, between the highest-ranking person attending and the quality of the departed's work (in this case Leslie). So far, no VP, maybe Leslie wasn't all that great.

Hugs are a big part of the going-away party. Look over there, Ross is on a collision course with Leslie. She was hoping for a catch-and-release hug, but Ross is squeezing a lot harder than he should and three seconds feel like an hour to her…you can see it on her face.

The ladies hug each other in a myriad of very considerate ways, usually complimenting clothing choices, or hair, or jewelry along the way. Some guys who are shy don't really want to hug Leslie but don't want to offend either, so they attempt awkward side hugs like two sixth graders stuck slow dancing at the school dance.

Suddenly, the highest-ranking people (VPs have arrived, Leslie *did* have skills) start clanging glasses with silverware. The requisite "KISS, KISS, KISS" unfunny joke comes flying out of not-so-funny sales guy who has clearly been to one too many weddings or had one too many drinks. He provides an enormous self-laugh…and then that moment is over as the crickets chirp in the background.

Suddenly the VP speaks for five to seven minutes about how amazing Leslie is. Another group provides a top 10 list of great moments in Leslie's career. And then Leslie tells everybody how much she loves them. And Leslie's last day is tomorrow.

CuBe TiPs

The going-away party is fraught with challenges. If handled right, it shows that the company DOES care about their employees, even in their final moments. Senior managers, you better believe every member of the soon-to-be-departed's current team and her closest friends in the company are seeing if you show up. If you do, morale improves or is neutral. If you don't, this can be a significantly negative morale

issue—make sure your business trip or vacation is well-publicized if you are out of town.

Don't get me wrong, I think going-away events are absolutely the right thing to do. I just think the "you still work here and are kicking butt and taking names" parties need to start happening more often. If the same creativity and energy put into going-away parties is put into "You Are Kicking Serious Butt and Taking Names" parties, good people are less likely to leave. Celebrate the peeps while they do work at your company, and they are much more likely to stay. Just sayin'.

Chapter 18

THE IMPORTANT DOCUMENTS

Expense Reports

The number one procrastinated item at the office (and number two is not even close) is the expense report. Filling them out stinks. If you manage others, you don't enjoy reviewing them either.

Some of you have pawned off compiling your expenses on your willing admin, who must make sense of your three-month-old wadded-up receipts (and they nail it every time). But, those without admin support are struggling with this, and it is a time and motivation drain. Let's go inside…

Amanda has a problem with expense reports. She feels like she should enroll in Expense Report Filler Outers Anonymous. She has made zero progress in her 14-year career. She simply refuses to fill out the forms in a timely, or for that matter, untimely fashion.

She even tries to protect herself from herself. She will put a 30-minute expense report meeting on her calendar, and then she doesn't show up for the meeting. She has no idea what she is doing, but she knows what she is not doing: filling out the form.

CuBe Tips

Look at the angst these forms are creating. You need to help your employees by getting tough—take on the persona of the meanest teacher you had in high school (anyone you remember who carried a ruler around as they taught). Demand that all expense reports from a trip must be turned in within one week or else...the ruler. Everyone benefits, trust me (joking about the ruler).

The Year-End Review

Some managers are simply not putting the time into delivering a quality year-end review. This review should be built on a series of conversations that have taken place throughout the year and should be void of surprises. Yet, many managers fill them out at the last minute to check a box with HR.

The other challenge with the reviews is the classifications people are placed in. Valued. Achieved expectations. These are the words some companies use to describe good, productive employees at their annual reviews.

That forces managers to say, "Phil, you had a really good year, not quite outstanding (two people in the ENTIRE company get that designation). You were right there where you need to be in the valued group. In fact, you were actually at the top end of valued; I'd call you Valued Plus." *BHT: Valued Plus sounds like new laundry detergent from Wal-Mart. "Valued Plus with amazing stain-fighting power."

Let's see what employees think by going INSIDE...

Ed thinks most managers treat reviews with pure disdain. He

thinks his manager does not spend nearly enough time on his. He would bet a $100 bill, a Benjamin, as the cool kids call them, that every one of his coworkers has heard a manager say: "Great, I have fifteen reviews to write, and they are due tomorrow."

Ed's manager has also canceled and postponed his annual review meeting three times because "I have a huge fire to put out." *BHT: unless you are truly hooking up a gigantic hose to a hydrant, no "fire" you have should be more important than Ed's annual review.

Cube Tips

Managers, the year-end review must be the most important meeting you conduct all year. Please treat these meetings with the same sense of importance and passion that you show when you are presenting your next big idea to senior executives. Your team is counting on you—it's the only way they are going to improve. Let them know that these meetings are THE top priority in your work schedule. If you want to be a great coach, it starts with commitment and feedback.

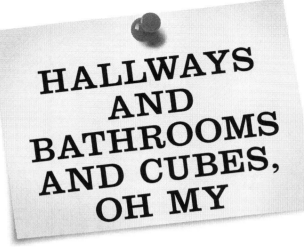

HALLWAYS AND BATHROOMS AND CUBES, OH MY

There is a variety of places people interact in the office. Some are private locations, while others are right out in the open. Regardless of the locale, it's how you interact with your colleagues in these settings that can have a lasting impact on your workplace's culture.

Chapter 19

HALLWAY CHATTER

When you move from place to place within your office, you are bound to have a variety of interactions in the hallway, many of which are quite awkward if you don't prepare. How you act in these situations can instantly affect morale and provide clues about you.

You cannot take the hallways for granted and you must be prepared with your "signature interaction move." You never know when you might see your best friend at work, your rival from another department, or come millimeters from slamming into the CEO who is carrying a full cup of hot coffee. Do you know what your move is?

HALLWAY STRANGER INTERACTION

You have to be so careful walking from meeting to meeting. From car to cube. From lunch to bathroom. Why? Well I assume you have no problems walking, but I will also assume that other human beings will be in the hallways as you navigate the halls. And this is a problem, because you have multiple chances to be the "rude guy," the "gross guy," or the "super happy girl" just based on how you interact when walking past people in the halls. Who you cross paths with and how you confront them can impact your morale instantly. Let's go INSIDE…

Greg is currently on his way to a meeting on the other side of the building. He is heading to a floor where he knows very few people, so he is certain to pass by someone he does not know. Sure enough, he sees a stranger dude coming toward him. He knows just how to play this one.

There is a move only guys can pull off that is so perfectly cordial. Greg needs to simply and swiftly lift his chin one and a half inches as you pass by the stranger dude. He will return the move toward Greg. Both parties have handled this interaction in a most cordial manner. *BHT: ladies, I'm not sure if you have a similar, non-verbal move you share with other stranger ladies in the hall, but at least you got a little insight into the world of men.

Greg can use another move that is available to both men and women. Just as he is entering the interaction point that would require a verbal interaction, he can pull that smart phone out of his pocket and stare a hole through that device as if he just got the most important text ever. The other person will never know that Greg was just looking at his lock screen.

Greg uses the iPhone to perfection and continues down the cube hallway. Suddenly, a coworker Greg kind of knows enters the flow of traffic walking in the same direction, so the two are traveling together until one of them takes an off ramp.

Greg fears silence and he has a very simplistic work relationship with his fellow walker, so he blurts out "staying out of trouble?" So awkward. *BHT: What response does Greg desire? "No, Greg, as a matter of fact, I robbed a bank last week and await my prison term."

Greg's companion bails toward another hallway, and he continues his journey to his desired meeting room. And, unfortunately for Greg, he has the worst hallway confrontation of all in front of him.

He thinks he sees a woman down the hall that he knows, and she waves. As Greg is in the middle of his wave (and also realizing that he doesn't know that person), he hears a female voice behind him say: "Hi Jenna, how are you?"

Greg is left with a check-swing hello, which he tries to turn into a quick head scratch that he thinks he got away with. That is, until Jenna's friend says "not so fast" and appeals Greg's check-swing hello to the third-base umpire, who says he went around and calls him out.

Finally, four steps from the door, Greg sees one of his work buddies who sits on his row. Greg is not sure why, but he salutes. And the salute is returned. Neither is a member of the military; they simply saluted because that was the best thing each could think of.

Greg walks in the meeting room, mentally exhausted.

C<small>U</small>B<small>E</small> T<small>I</small>P<small>S</small>

Stranger-infested hallways can be as terrifying as shark-infested waters at the height of tourist season. Have a plan to be nice, to be cordial, and to know your options. And if all else fails, please just smile (not awkward), but a real "nice to see you" smile.

O<small>H</small>, <small>THE</small> W<small>AY</small> W<small>E</small> T<small>ALK</small>: T<small>HE</small> S<small>IZE</small> <small>OF</small> Y<small>OUR</small> W<small>EEKEND</small> P<small>LANS</small>

Friday afternoons are very interesting in the office. Most of the time, people are generally happy. Groups are gathered in the halls and leaning, Ziggy-like, over the cubicles chatting. And the number one question posed back and forth in these afternoon huddles is: "Got any big plans this weekend?"

Why is everybody putting so much pressure on the size of their coworker's plans? No one ever asks if you have any medium plans this weekend, or heaven forbid, the most egregious small plans? No, you must have big plans.

The problem with this line of questioning is that no one has produced a chart that shows what it is you need to be doing to qualify for "BIG PLANS." Is flying dolphin- and shark-shaped kites with your family BIG PLANS? Or do you have to involve Shamu in the equation to qualify?

The Bolt at Five Bells

The hallways at your office are life threatening at five o'clock, especially if you are near the elevators. Let's go INSIDE…

Kyle works from eight to five. Not eight to 5:02. Eight to five. At 4:58, he is gearing up to enter the starting blocks like Usain Bolt getting ready to run the 100-yard dash. Instead of stretching out his hamstrings, he is shutting down his computer, packing up his backpack and lunch-carrying device, and getting ready for the starting "gun" to go off.

He waits for his own personal official time-keeping device (iPhone time for Kyle) to switch from 4:59:59 to 5:00:00 and then good-bye, workplace. At 5:00:00 p.m., he leaps from his cubicle like the eight finalists in the Olympic 100-meter finals.

CuBe TiPs

The challenge for you is that these sprinters are not contained to their 48-inch-wide lanes within in a stadium—they are loose within the narrow halls and corridors of your office. It is like Pamplona in the springtime if you find yourself loose in the hallway with the sprinters. Please, for your own personal health and safety, if you find yourself roaming the office at this hour, grab some wall and remain absolutely still. Do NOT, I repeat, do NOT go near the elevators at this hour, your safety cannot be guaranteed.

OH, THE THINGS WE SAY: THE WRONG DIRECTION

Silence is indeed golden. The need to talk often creates problems. Sometimes we just feel compelled to talk when we see another human being. We can't help ourselves. And this creates awkward moments that would have been easy to avoid.

Picture the scene: Janet is leaving the office a bit late one night, around 6:55. She is 15 steps from the exit door to the parking lot when, suddenly, one of her coworkers, Ben, opens the door and is walking into the office. One hundred out of 100 times this situation follows the same pattern.

The brain of every office worker in America processes this situation the same way. EVERY SINGLE TIME, the person leaving (in this case Janet) will immediately blurt out: "Going the wrong way, Ben." And there is tone in that statement. There is more than a hint of "my direction is so much better than *your* direction."

Let's not have this conversation anymore. Just keep walking. You both are at the office late tonight. Of course you can be polite and throw an "Evenin', Ben" at him. But whatever you do, don't start a conversation. Because then you are both stuck in a 20-second chat of supreme awkwardness that neither of you really want. And maybe Ben just forgot his keys.

THE ENTRY STRATEGY & THE ZAMBONI EXIT

You must plan for the days you might hit the snooze button three extra times, because you know and I know that there will be mornings when that happens (like that first really cold morning in the fall when the sheets are freezing cold and you are bundled up in three layers of blankets and it is pure nirvana and that 8:30 meeting can just freakin' wait). You will be late on some days—it's just going to happen. Because traffic happens. Because hunger happens. Because life happens. And because the snooze button happens. And because you will be confronted with these obstacles on many mornings, it's how you handle it that's critical. Let's go INSIDE…

Nancy knows that people in her office are paying attention to when she arrives and when she leaves (regardless of the fact that these people are not her boss, or even on her team). Mental notes are being taken. People know if Nancy is an 8:20 to 5:30 or an 8:00 to 4:30 person. The perception of her work hours bugs Nancy, even though she knows it really doesn't matter, at all, to her boss.

This morning, Nancy had a snooze moment. Luckily for her she has worked on an entry strategy that gets her to her cube by walking past the least amount of people possible. She hits the door of her office with focus and a plan. She knows she MUST avoid all large conference rooms with glass windows, her boss's boss's office, and the break room—non-negotiable.

She knows that one of the senior VP's office is hard to avoid without hurdling the corner of one cube, so she does hurdles it like a pro—nothing to see here. Her final move is to go up and down a flight of stairs that avoid a high-traffic area and ease into her desk.

She now acts like she has been working at her desk for quite some time (every night, and last night was no exception, she disabled any and all startup sounds on her computer for times just like these). Two years ago, she nailed her route to her desk, and then the Windows startup sounds came blaring out of her computer because she cranked a YouTube video the night before.

She practices this route about once a quarter on days when she is not late, to ensure the muscle memory. She does not like the stress of being late, but she is especially relieved this morning when her previously mapped out alternative arrival route got her to her cube with zero human interaction.

When Nancy is leaving late, she knows it is time to be seen and she plays to the crowd. She is not proud of it, but to satisfy her inner need to get credit from the clock-watchers, she will pull a Zamboni exit. She will get that entire ice surface cleaned by going up and down each row of cubes.

She says good night to everybody. She waves her hands like she's riding on the Rose Parade float that won the Governor's Cup Award. She absolutely pops into the break room on her way out. And as the kind, cordial person that she is, she pokes her head into the VP's office and says good night (if she is in there, that was one powerful poke).

DO NOT OVERUSE THIS MOVE, but a monthly Zamboni exit can go a long, long way.

Cube Tips

Perception IS reality in the minds of many people, especially those that have a strong desire to please. If you are one of these people, try to contain your obsession and remind yourself that it is ultimately your work, not your workday start time, that will impact your career growth. Channel your creativity into solving business problems, not designing entry and exit routes.

Chapter 20

PUT MY FOCUS IN [BRACKETS]

Over 60% of office workers say they fill out an NCAA tournament bracket according to online polls. Three million people spend one to three hours at work watching the NCAA basketball tournament at work according to a *Huffington Post* article. Let's go INSIDE…

It's the morning of the NCAA basketball tourney. And in row after row of cubes, colleges like Florida Atlantic, Bucknell, and Gonzaga are being discussed with such fervor you'd think you were at an alumni rally for each school.

Brian, the resident college basketball expert, is sitting there with three brackets that he believes are as perfect as they get (although just admitting three different things are perfect is in and of itself contradictory). He is holding court about the hardwood court, providing a dissertation on the Syracuse zone defense and the athleticism of the Kansas backcourt.

There is a group of 10 people around him who have not watched one second of college basketball all year. But the bracket sheet they each have in front of them is now the single most important item at the workplace. They ask questions, Brian answers, they fill in more lines of the brackets. Some just pick the nearby schools, or the states, or the mascot names (as if they even know those). But they are invested.

Lindsey tells Brian that he HAS to fill out her bracket so she can beat her husband. With Brian's help, she can "stick it to her husband." Brian grabs a pen and dutifully fills out Lindsey's bracket. He gives her most of his upset specials, but keeps his favorite bracket to himself. He loves the attention, you can tell.

Every office has that one person that organizes the contests. At this office, it is the rock star admin, Judy. Judy is going up and down the rows of cubes making sure everyone gets their entries in on time. College names are being yelled from cube to cube. And unlike the passion shown for specific teams during college football season, these names merely finalize a job. Wichita State? OK, fine. Wichita State it is, moving along now. Nothing else to see here; must finish the West regional in the next five minutes.

Once the tourney starts, the scene looks much different. Certainly Brian is monitoring every game, some of the big college basketball fans are watching parts of games online between meetings, and those that had made the bracket their number one priority earlier in the day have merely pinned it to the side of their most-of-a-cube and moved on with their lives. They will check it that night, but mission critical was simply playing. They have a bracket. And having a bracket, no matter how right or wrong it is, is a good thing. Bragging rights, whether within the office itself or, in Lindsey's case, at home, can be earned.

CuBe TiPs

The NCAA basketball tournament is a tremendous morale booster if done right. If a fun contest like the NCAA tourney with a small entry fee is OK at your office (and my opinion is that it should be), then you

should absolutely participate and encourage others to do so. Tracking the teams and the brackets is a great way for you to improve relationships with others in the office who you may not know that well (who knew that Justin in Accounting also went to Butler).

If you desire to be the catalyst for culture and morale in your office, organize the bracket challenge. All of the major online sports sites offer free pools, so there is very little organization that you need to do—but you will reap the rewards of leading positive culture. Plus, you will get to say and learn fun words like "Billikens," "Bearcats," and "Boilermakers."

Chapter 21

TRUST & RESPECT

The people. The others. You will develop some of your best friendships with your work colleagues. Lifetime friends. You will develop your core group that you can count on. You will have those you get along with. There will probably be a few that you don't connect with, but you have to find a way to trust and respect them.

The challenge is that when the human resources are all confined in small places called cubicles, all share a bathroom, a kitchen, and a dining room, trouble is bound to happen. The better we communicate, the better we share, the better we act, the better our morale will be.

DON'T TICK OFF BETTY

I have one simple suggestion for those of you starting new jobs, working in a new department, or even getting new admin support in your current job: Don't Tick Off Betty. Everything starts and stops there. Let's go INSIDE…

Colby is eager to get off to a good start at his new company, ready to blaze a trail of success in his new job at his new office.

Colby straddles that cocky/confident line and can often be seen on the cocky side.

At the beginning, Colby is doing some great work, but he is leaving a trail of wreckage behind his work. He is extremely respectful of senior leadership (almost too respectful), but he treats his admin, Betty, like his own personal errand runner.

Suddenly he can't seem to get his computer to work just right. He's having trouble getting meetings set up with key executives. And his company credit card still hasn't come in.

Do you know why? He thought the SVP or CEO was the most important person at the company, but he was wrong. Dead wrong. Betty is the department admin who runs this show—she is at the top of the org chart. Colby ticked off Betty.

CuBe TiPs

Forging relationships with your coworkers is an essential ingredient of a successful career. Many forget the most important people—the tremendous admins at offices across the country who make so many people look so good.

If you see Betty in the hallway, you MUST give her a huge greeting, just shy of creepy, every time. You better know the stuff she loves. And you better be able to have a conversation with her when you bump into her in the break room. If you tick off Betty, you will not be successful. Toss the career aspirations into the fire pit. Betty will NOT get you the meeting room you need (nor should she—you must respect her). Betty is, by FAR, the most important person in the building. The less successful peeps treat her poorly. Do not follow in these footsteps. Get to know Betty. She's cool. Really cool.

OH, THE THINGS WE SAY: FINAL FINAL

So you are walking by a group of people gathered around a printed piece. One of them, in a very animated state, asks, "Well is it final final?" If it was just single final, would that mean that changes could still be made because it hadn't made it to the even more final, level two final final? What are we doing and saying?

Stop the madness. Do not perpetuate these abuses of the English language. Yes, the definition of final is "ultimate, conclusive, or decisive." No need to double or triple up on it. Call your coworkers out when they start with office speak, or else we'll never know when something really is finished. Is that deck finished finished?

THE OVERUSE OF CORPORATE CATCHPHRASES

Some folks latch onto corporate catchphrases and use them as a part of their daily vocabulary. Some use them because they heard the VP say it. Others use them to get ahead (at least they think that way). Let's go INSIDE…

Vince is always dropping names and using the corporate catchphrase of the day. He can't help himself; it's how he's wired. He left this message last night for a cross-functional partner:

"Hey Bob, on the ball bearings project, let's make sure we are all on the same page because at the end of the day, there are no bad ideas. let's look at this from forty thousand feet moving forward. So if you can circle back and touch base with me to make sure we set up a parking lot to capture anything that comes up in a hallway conversation that would be great. And if you can put a bug in Mike's ear to get the ball rolling that would be terrific because the gatekeepers are expecting us to over deliver. And if we fail…it may be with mixed emotions that your boss announces that you left the company to pursue other opportunities."

CuBe TiPs

Corporate catchphrases gone wild can destroy morale and create animosity between coworkers. You can shut down this "bullying via thesaurus" behavior by calling out people who speak without truly saying anything. And make sure that you are not participating. Don't repeatedly say "at the end of the day" around 6:00pm, because guess what, it's already arrived.

THE SIT & RUN IN BROAD DAYLIGHT

An office is a confined place where you come in contact with other human beings who may have germs, diseases, and questionable hygiene. In fact, you may be one of the folks who go to great lengths to avoid coworker germs. Let's go INSIDE...

Trey is a known germaphobe, especially in the bathroom. In here, he would not be able to function without his elbows. Watch as he flushes with his elbows, as he turns on the faucet with his elbows, and see how he accesses the paper towels with his elbows. No fingers or opposable thumbs are involved.

When he exits the bathroom, do you think he lets human flesh touch the door handle? Absolutely not. He must take an extra piece of paper towel with him as he heads out of the bathroom and use it as a safety barrier on the handle.

Trey is especially focused on his "elbow routine" in the bathroom because of an instance a couple of months ago. Trey was standing there at the sinks, washing his hands. The stalls are to his left. The door to his right.

As he washed his hands, he heard a click that certainly came from that flimsy yet so important piece of metal that holds the stall door shut. He then saw a vision of a human being flash directly behind him to his right… and out the door.

This individual pulled a sit and run, in broad daylight. The handle was now untouchable, full of a vile infection. Trey took a deep breath, made an eight-ply paper towel glove, and escaped the office bathroom that day, disgusted. And now he fears that handle.

C_uB_e T_iP_s

OK, the purpose of this section is not to be gross. It's to point out the impact poor hygiene can have on morale and productivity. If you see egregious bathroom behavior, you will absolutely be distracted after it occurs. You might even feel the need to tell some of your closest coworkers about what you just saw. It's not productive. So try to treat the office bathroom with the same approach you do with the ones in your home.

OH, THE THINGS WE SAY: THE PERFECT ATTENDANCE RIBBON

You are sitting there at your desk, and your cube mate, Jackie, comes laboring by you and sits down. She is sniffling. She is coughing. In five minutes she has exhausted her entire box of Kleenex. Jackie is a workaholic and always comes into the office. When describing her malady, she says she has the flu and 103-degree fever.

Jackie then states, "You probably don't want to get too close to me today." Well, guess what. You drew the lucky straw today because your cube touches Jackie's and there is no way to avoid her. Nor can the people in the meetings she attends in close quarters, or the people she might hack on in the break room.

*BHT: To these people I say STOP. You had us at "flu." We are not giving out perfect attendance ribbons. Tell the world you are working from home and rip off 100 e-mails from your laptop in the prone position on your living room couch while you watch *The Price is Right*. But please, don't bring your contagious sickness into the office.

Chapter 22

MOST-OF-A-CUBE

You need a place, a location, a plot of land to perform your work. Most companies bequeath dwellings to their employees. These dwellings are called cubes. All "cubes" you have encountered in your life probably have full sides and a top. To be more specific, you likely work in "most-of-a-cube."

This is your spot to personalize, to put your stamp on the decoration. To show the world what you are all about in an 8' x 8' space. In larger companies, you get assigned an address like 3C224. Privacy is tough to find, and at an absolute premium if located. Picture your most-of-a-cube and visualize the vibe it portrays about you, your life, and your work style.

OH, THE THINGS WE DO: THE PRAIRIE DOGS

When you are sitting there in your most-of-a-cube and you hear a crash three rows over, your head (and those of your coworkers) pop up like a bunch of prairie dogs. You yell: "Are you all right? Are you OK?" And then you always exaggerate it. "Do I need to call 9-1-1?" You assume it's all clear or an ambulance is needed RFN.

Or, if you hear a baby a few cubes over, up pop the prairie dogs again. "It's Janet's bay-bee. Oh, she's so cute. *Hiii!*" The shorter people are trying to get a peek but can't see so they are trying to balance on their office chair. This is a horrible idea…please get off the chair and walk around or you WILL need an ambulance for yourself.

CUBESDROPPING

Your most-of-a-cube street is a shared space. You can hear everything that's going on around you. Let's go INSIDE…

Sarah sits right in the middle of a very busy row in her workplace. Right now, there are multiple conversations going on all around her. To her left is a sales guy who enjoys holding conference calls at his desk, on the speaker phone, with the volume CRANKED. Sarah is so distracted that she has considered pulling up a chair and sitting next to him. She's already on the call; she might as well have better seats.

Later in the day, it's 4:30 and there's the crazy family coordination that is going on in the cube behind Sarah. She hears: "Ok, Joey's got soccer at five, so if you can drop him off at the field and get Tina to ballet by six and if you can get a rotisserie chicken for dinner…" Sarah actually got a good idea from this bit of cubesdropping because rotisserie chicken dinner doesn't sound too bad.

But the call she wants to hear most is the call that just started to her right. "Is Dr. Gordon available?" got Sarah's immediate attention. She knows she cannot talk now. She takes out her earphones. She stops typing. Because even though she can only hear half of the conversation, she wants to hear every single word. What if the word "contagious" comes up? She wants to know what he's got.

CUBE TIPS

When you are on a call at your desk, just assume that everyone around you is too. If it's a personal call, then find a more private spot where you can talk openly with your doctor. If you are on a work call, try

not to use that speaker button at your desk; it's really rude to do so. And if you are surrounded by some loud peeps, invest in some Beats by Dre—good earphones can instantly improve your morale as you crank through a project at your desk with your favorite music in crystal-clear clarity in your ears, oblivious to the coworkers all around you.

CUBE ADORNMENTS

Lots of crazy stuff gets places on cube walls. You see photographs, cute drawings from the kids, sports team memorabilia. Let's go INSIDE...

Nita needed to pay Joe a visit to discuss a work project. On her way to his cube, she encountered one coworker who displayed beautiful collages of her kids and the family...from six years ago. Most photographs in the office are from the first week a person started at the office. No effort is being made to update these pictures—the "toddlers" in this collage are now teenagers.

In the cube next to Joe's, Nita notices a GPS tracking note and itinerary taped to the computer monitor. It's their way of letting everyone at the office know where they are in case of a natural disaster. If it's a business trip, the writing is small. However, Nita is staring at a vacation note. It says: "I AM IN HAWAII FROM 5/4–5/13" in gigantic, break room, fridge-clean-out-threat font.

Nita finally arrives at Joe's cube, and there he is. But does Joe know that Nita is there? Nope. Joe sits with his back to those entering his cube.

Do you know what he has done to solve this little predicament? He has paid a visit to the auto industry and installed a rearview mirror above his desk. Guess he can see the rapidly approaching traffic. In a panic, he must be unbelievable at alt-tabbing to a work related page.

CuBe TiPs

When you are not at your desk, you are likely to have visitors. They will check out your photos. They will review the décor. They will search for a "sticky" so they can leave you a note. And if you choose to sit with your back to the most-of-a-cube entry point, you are forfeiting your last possible shot at privacy. Review other desk/computer layouts, and you just might boost your morale by a simple three-foot move of your computer.

Bad Hygiene Decision Andy

Some people are going to perform acts at their desk that will infuriate you. Let's go INSIDE…

There's a gentleman on the third floor that has received, due to his own poor behavior, a most debilitating nickname. He is known as Bad Hygiene Decision Andy. He flosses at his desk. But that is not the worst thing that Andy does. Andy clips his freakin' nails at his desk. The sound is excruciating.

But what his cube neighbors are worried about is the shrapnel. Because every time he cuts his nails, the stuff's flying everywhere. You know his right hand is probably pretty good, but his left hand is likely terrible, creating sharper, more dangerous pieces. When Andy is loose in the office with a potentially deadly weapon, there is little chance for a morale boost or improved productivity.

CuBe TiPs

There is NEVER a good reason to clip your nails at your desk. EVER.

LABOR DAY

You probably know by now that at Freeman+Leonard we consider Labor Day our favorite holiday. It's the one day each year that our country honors the people who really make things happen, the American workforce. Our business is helping clients solve marketing and advertising challenges with the very people who know how best to do just that. Everyone wins. Our clients get great marketing communications solutions. Our talent gets the opportunity to work with great clients.

We want to thank you for your business this past year by sharing a light-hearted read from a big-hearted talent. Dave Fleming is a work-place humorist. His book, *Inside the Cubicle*, explores the universal, yet funny, insights of office behavior, communications and morale. So grab a coffee from the break room, prop your feet up on your desk and prepare to get a good chuckle as you discover what *really* affects the people in your office.

And, as you're enjoying Dave's book, please know that we appreciate your business.

Sincerely,

Kathy Leonard
President
kleonard@freemanleonard.com

THE PRIVACY PROBLEM

Privacy is tough to come by in today's office environment. As previously mentioned, cube heights are down, everyone is assigned "most-of-a-cube" and expected to go about their business. And for the business end of this arrangement, this lack of privacy is fine. But, you see, life keeps happening all around work. Let's go INSIDE...

It's not hard to tell when someone is on a personal call at work. Look at Jackie over there. Three minutes ago she was talking in her normal voice about some invoices or some other business issue. And then her phone rang and she became a low talker. She is literally ducking down below her low cube walls and trying to disappear. Now she has wedged herself into the corner of her cube and is basically rolled up into a ball, with the phone in the midst of this somewhere. Obviously, some life issue appeared on the other end of the line and there is Jackie, in her most-of-a-cube, trying to deal with it.

Now look over here, in the stairwell. Yes, that's Kevin in the stairwell. I'm pretty sure Kevin doesn't WANT to be in the stairwell, but he's in the stairwell, on his cell phone, because life came up in the middle of his workday. So, he had to find some privacy. And on this hot day, he decided to head to the part of the building without air conditioning. It also has relatively poor cell reception, and a fairly consistent string of people going from floor to floor in the office. Watch him pace back and forth in that little landing area between flights of stairs, ignoring his coworkers as if he's in a soundproof booth. This was Kevin's number one choice to have this call because life entered his workday.

And look over there. Steve is on the phone in his cube. He appears to be talking to his wife about the day's events. He is clearly getting some instructions for his role in the evening's family agenda. A honey-do list that includes picking up honeydew melon for dinner. He has been talking at a normal volume level, even laughing on occasion, and just as the call appears to be wrapping up, he cups his hand over his mouth and whispers, "I love you." For Steve, that was a private moment not to be shared, so he acted like an offensive coordinator calling in the plays from the sideline with the laminated play sheet in front of his mouth so the opponent cannot read his lips.

CuBe Tips

It is time to make it easier for people to deal with life issues at work. It should not be this hard to have some privacy. In most office settings today, very few people have doors. So let's create the communal door. Assign one small room with a door on every floor of every office as the "LIFE" room. I'm not talking about setting up a Facebook lounge where everyone can keep up with the day's posts—I'm talking about a place to go when you need to talk about doctors and other family issues. And let's not judge people who go in and out of there. And it should always be OK to say "I love you" at your normal speaking volume (and a couple of volume numbers higher).

Meals are really hard at work, especially lunch. You might eat every day with your "work wife" or "work husband." You might always sit at the "sports table" or with the "younger group." You might be the one that always goes out for lunch. Whatever the case, you have to plan.

Morale can be damaged if your lunch is stolen, if a group leaves without you for a local sandwich shop, or if you simply forgot your lunch on the kitchen table. When, what, where, and with whom—this is your daily dining dilemma.

Chapter 23

THE HUNGER GAMES

THE LUNCH DATE

Lunch is as close as most of us get to dating our coworkers. Let's go INSIDE…

Doug is sitting there at his desk at 9:00 a.m. He knows he only has a few hours to drum up some lunch plans. He is not usually part of one of the groups that always eat at the same time in the same spot. And he doesn't have a "work wife" who he can count on for lunch every day. The other day, Doug's morale was damaged because four of his closest work friends went to Chick-fil-Aa without him.

Doug also knows he cannot afford to eat out every day. It doesn't make sense. He will mix in the occasional PB&J. But on this day, he has no food and no one to eat with. It's now 9:04 and he is chasing lunch dates with men and women so he is not stuck eating alone at a local fast food spot.

Cube Tips

Do not let your lunch plans consume your work morning. Many people choose to eat lunch at their desk. But remember it is poor form to rummage through the fridge. Do check out the break room table. Maybe you'll strike gold because somebody ordered way too much pizza.

Oh, the Things We Do: Poor Microwave Behavior

When you are heating up leftovers, there is a simple rule. If it stunk in YOUR kitchen last night, imagine adding that smell to the burned popcorn and other skunk-like smells that can dominate the break room. I'm begging you: leave that stuff at home.

If you do use the microwave, let's see some courtesy. You brought a microwaveable dish, so you need to babysit it. Bring your smart phone in the break room and catch up on e-mail—make this a productive time. You cannot hit start and walk away.

Do not set it to cook for five minutes and return twenty minutes later. Two things will happen after that buzzer sounds indicating the five minutes is up: (1) your lunch will be long gone because the next in line will have pulled it out and put it on the break room table (and an item on the break room table without a name on it is up for grabs, or in this case, likely gone); (2) if that next someone in line is Betty, wondering who abandoned their lunch, guess what you did—yep, you ticked her off. BAD MOVE.

The Noon Meeting Food Quandary

When a meeting falls on your calendar from noon to one, it is many things. It's a bit rude. It was probably the only time all parties were free. And it is a food decision disaster. Let's go INSIDE...

Dayna doesn't know how to deal with the noon meeting on her calendar today. Because she has to answer the key question: Is there likely to be food based on the attendees and the subject matter? She checks the invite and sees a senior VP in attendance, so she figures she can count on pizza at the bare minimum. At last week's budget reconciliation with her peers, however, there was no food in sight.

Dayna's interest in attending noon meetings is quite low if there is no free lunch associated with it. But, if there is a deli tray in the mix, with some salad, a couple of bags of chips, and some pop, she's eager and ready.

Dayna heads to the noon meeting room and her pizza expectation is not met. There is NOTHING, zero, zip, zilch placed on that one auxiliary table that sits to the side of the main meeting table; you know, where the lunch fixings should be.

She takes a quick survey of the peeps at the table, all stuffing their faces with their own little homemade delights or menu items from the café purchased 10 minutes ago. How did THEY know? It's 11:59, there is no deli tray, and she has no shot at food for the next 60–120 minutes. Her interest in this meeting is now equal to the amount of free food she will receive.

CUBE TIPS

There is a simple way to be a hero to everyone in the office. Institute a policy. If you call a noon meeting, you MUST provide lunch for all in attendance. Those do-gooders working during lunch for your meeting will be happy, well fed, and focused. Remember, if FREE is marketed properly, it is a powerful four-letter word.

Chapter 24

BIRTHDAYS MAKE US ACT LIKE WHOS

Birthday celebrations are full of secret service covert operations. Let's go INSIDE…

Betty is in charge of getting cards for everyone's birthday. She has to hide that card from the birthday boy—there is no way he is going to make visual contact with that Hallmark treasure. Because he has no way of knowing that it's his birthday and he might get a card—that is TOP SECRET information.

Betty hides it in the special purple file folder and sneaks past the birthday boy's desk ("nothing to see here") to get the signing process started.

Even the decoration of the most-of-a-cube is a big secret. They wait until the birthday boy leaves the office, then the decorating committee comes out of nowhere with streamers, tape, balloons, and helium tanks. And these committees love the "happy birthday confetti"—they throw glittery red-and-blue "Happys" and "Birthdays" all over the place (which are IMPOSSIBLE to clean up). There is no doubt that the birthday boy will find a hidden "Birthday" in seven months.

The birthday card lands on Jamie's desk. She treats it the same way she treated the yearbook back in high school. She reads what everybody else wrote first. And on this occasion, the group did NOT care to send its very best. They are just mailing it in. There are four "happy b-days" and five "have a good ones." The reason is simple—there is no free food associated with this birthday yet.

BUT, at a predetermined time, the group gathers back in the break room and forms a perimeter much like the Whos did around their Christmas tree in Whoville. The only difference between this group and the Whos is that they usually don't hold hands.

Then there is a stare down. Will there be singing? Is someone gonna get the song started? Suddenly, a type A salesman who is craving some sugar starts up the most awful rendition of "Happy Birthday" you have ever heard. The group gets through it and everybody gets cake. It's truly a happy birthday.

CuBe TiPs

First, make sure there *is* a committee that does the decorating. Second, make sure there *is* a list of birthdays so no one is forgotten (yes, a birthday can suddenly be a morale destroyer). Third, if there is a gift, and you are funding via the chip-in, make it a small amount. Don't make people feel uncomfortable comparing what they spent on a coworker to what they spent on their sweet Aunt Rose. Fourth, do not mess up the cake. People might say they like carrot cake, but they don't like it nearly as much as they like chocolate cake. Do NOT go rogue—chocolate cake plus butter cream icing is a guaranteed winner for all.

This final section comes directly from my life and my career (thus the title of the section—thanks, genius). The prior sections came directly from what I have seen, what I have observed, and what I have researched at workplaces across the country. But this chapter is different. This chapter is my chance to share some of my personal stories that helped drive my own personal morale, while inspiring others.

My hope for this section is for you to laugh, learn, and then go lead your organization with a new perspective gained from what I have experienced.

Chapter 25

A PRESIDENT PRACTICES PASSION

Most of this book is focused on observations that universally apply to the workplace, regardless of the size or type of business. But I also wanted to go INSIDE my career and share some specific experiences that can impact your morale and communication skills. In our careers, we interact with many people. The president of the first company I worked for after college is the impetus for many learning experiences. Let's go INSIDE:

In my first job out of college, I worked at a dental insurance company that was just starting to form a marketing department. The job market was horrible, the salary was lousy, but I signed up, ready to embark on a career. But as a passionate guy, where in the world do I find passion in dental insurance?

OK, it's easy to admit that designing brochures about "improving your dental hygiene" and "proper flossing techniques" is not exactly stimulating. So the product (or in this case, the service) alone was not delivering the passion.

What about the work itself? At a young age, I got to do the following: manage a six-figure budget, work directly with the president of the company, lead and choose our sales team tracking software, be the key contact with our advertising agency, and be on set for the filming of a TV commercial. So, while it was like pulling teeth (#awfulpun) to get passionate about the service we provided as an entity by itself, I could certainly get excited about how I was marketing the product.

So package the experience I was getting with the service, and I became quite the passionate dental insurance marketer. I looked for ways to differentiate our service from the competition. For our company was not about teeth, we were about making it easy for you to take advantage of a benefit provided to you by your employer.

You can find passion anywhere; some people are born with it. Some people need to be coddled and pushed to find it. And some rebel against it. Again, dental insurance and passion are not usually connected…but then you never met the president of the company I worked for—we'll call him Tony.

When you work for a man with a vocabulary bigger than Roget's and an ego bigger than Trump's, you have your hands full. It was not OK for me to call him Tony. It was Mr. Thomas to me and everyone else in the company. But this guy truly loved the industry, and he loved the David vs. Goliath challenge that was the reality of our business model.

You see, our company sold but one thing, dental insurance. The big bad behemoths like Blue Cross/Blue Shield packaged dental insurance with the more critical and more expensive medical insurance, offering one-stop shopping. Mr. Thomas saw this as an opportunity, not a problem.

So, he set forth to form the best dental insurance company he possibly could. Our company would be the little guy who could provide dental insurance 50 times better than the big guys. "Go ahead and use their expertise for the medical part of your benefits package, Mr. HR Director, but carve out the dental insurance for us, the experts." He worked feverishly on the RTBs (Reasons To Believe) of his message: fast claims service, unparalleled dentist network, and fair, competitive prices.

Our company grew every year I was there, because of the passion of Mr. Thomas. Mr. Thomas was a workaholic but legitimately wanted us to succeed, and I was the beneficiary of seeing a visionary at a young age. I was also at the mercy of deciphering English words as if he was speaking another language.

At the aforementioned television ad shoot, Mr. Thomas did not like the way the male actor was pronouncing the word "insurance." He said that the actor had a sibilant s. What? "Yes, he most definitely has a sibilant s," he insisted. I thought to myself, "I don't know what kind of s I have, but I sure don't want it to be sibilant."

Now this was before Al Gore invented the Internet, so I had to find a dictionary. I quickly looked up sibilant, which is defined as: "Characterized by having a hissing sound." Yep, this actor was hissing the s in "insurance" on nearly every take. Most people would have said he seems to be struggling with the pronunciation of his s, But Mr. Thomas dropped "sibilant" in our laps.

So it has probably bugged you that I keep referring to this cat as Mr. Thomas (hopefully not). But to be clear, it bugged me and my coworkers quite a bit. So, I'll let you in on a little secret...I got to call him Tony on four occasions. The four times I went golfing with him. You see, on the course, away from his kingdom, Tony was in play. It wasn't announced, and if you were new to the group, you just kind of caught on. I'd even crack myself up a little by putting just a bit more of an accent than necessary on the *Tony* at the end of simple golf compliments—"That's a nice drive, *TONY*"—picture Julia Louis Dreyfus in *Christmas Vacation* saying, "Why is the carpet all wet, *TODD*?"

Tony was not a good athlete (not that you need to be a good athlete to be a good golfer, but it helps). But he was as passionate about golf as he was about dental insurance. He understood his strengths and weaknesses and was happy to hit two shorter, straighter shots while others killed the ball and chased them in the woods. His score got better each year, and he played passionately every time he put one of our company's logoed golf balls onto one of our company's logoed tees.

Cube Tips

Passion is contagious. It inspires performance and improves morale. If you are in a leadership position and can pour your passion out in a way your team can see it, everyone will benefit.

A foil or adversary can drive morale. Tony didn't care about the size of his company versus the competition. He looked for a way to rally the troops against entities 10 times his size. He never apologized for being the underdog, he embraced it. And in his personal life, he saw his golf handicap as the "enemy" and focused on improving that number each year.

Finally, despite the good stuff Tony did, it is weird not to use your first name at work. Really weird. And a bit condescending. OK, VERY condescending. At your office, no matter what level you attain, don't be a Mr. Thomas (or a Mr. or Mrs. Anything). But do watch *Christmas Vacation* each holiday season to enjoy Todd and Margo and all of the Griswold clan.

Chapter 26

A STRONG FIRST IMPRESSION

This is the story of how one job interview left a lifelong impression on me. Let's go INSIDE…

I wanted to reinvigorate my marketing career with a fun company and a fun industry. As I started my search, I found a listing for a "Field Marketing Manager" job for Pizza Hut in Phoenix. It sounded (and likely tasted) good.

Little did I know that my work in college (at Miami University) would come in handy. You see, one of the projects of our marketing club was to promote the local Pizza Hut in town. We did fundraisers, coupons, and even built a huge slice of pizza in the back of a red pickup truck as a "float" in the homecoming parade.

That slice of pizza got me in the door, because I had actual experience doing what this Pizza Hut marketing job required. So I got the interview and flew to LA to meet with the director of the position. She oozed passion and wanted the same from her new hire. We had much more of a creative conversation than a formal job interview. She saw that I really wanted the job and had a lot to offer. I saw a passionate person I could learn from who would likely be an amazing boss.

At the end of the interview, she called the driver who was taking me back to the airport in Orange County and said, "Make sure you take the scenic route." I didn't know exactly what that meant, but 10 minutes later as we drove along the splendor of the Pacific Ocean, I certainly knew. It would have been easy to take the most direct route back to the airport, but this was the whipped cream on the sundae of an amazing first impression with one stellar view.

CuBe TiPs

You just never know how the dots in your life will connect. A small task done well can lead to a big opportunity later in life. For me, a huge wooden slice of pepperoni pizza in a parade in Oxford, OH, led me to Phoenix (just let that sink in).

First impressions are long lasting. That Pizza Hut director left an impression on me that I will never forget. Simple, thoughtful gestures can carry huge weight. Always be on the lookout for the "scenic route" when trying to make a positive impact on another person's life.

Chapter 27

MAY THE FORCE BE WITH ME

I got the job at Pizza Hut. My first day on the job was quite memorable. Go INSIDE, let us…

I was Obi Wan Kenobi on my first day on the job at Pizza Hut. Lightsaber, check. Robe, check. Cool, long, gray-haired wig…check. We're talking the older, cooler, original Obi Wan. The Alec Guiness Obi Wan. I was Obi Wan, I felt the FORCE; I just didn't have the cool accent Sir Alec brought to the role. And I wasn't exactly on set with George Lucas directing me, either.

I was actually on a stage at a community center in Phoenix, at midnight, on my first day on the job at Pizza Hut. Pizza Hut is one of the companies that make up Yum Brands, and the tradition of culture and recognition certainly are not just centrally located in the home office (or RSC, as they call it—Restaurant Support Center). If the message isn't felt, lived, and breathed in the field, then the pursuit is a failure. All organization charts at Pizza Hut place the Restaurant General Manager (RGM) at the top. All efforts must ultimately make their life better. The Phoenix market embodied that vision…thus the lightsabers.

At this late-night ride on a faux Millennium Falcon, I was not asked to present some elaborate marketing plans I had never seen before. I was merely there to be introduced, to show the team that they had a new marketing person to support them. And I wanted to show them I was willing to do whatever it took to help them win. I was set up for success on my first day (and maybe some wisdom from Yoda seeped into my head as well, who knows).

Now, why on earth were we all decked out in *Star Wars* gear in the first place (Darth, Luke, Leia, Han, Chewy were all represented by various cross-functional leaders)? And why that hour of the night? Pizza Hut was a huge sponsor of the release of Episode I, the Phantom Menace.

It was critical that the restaurants executed some very un-pizza like things—there was a consumer game, there were toys to sell, there were passionate fans to accommodate. It was also critical that ALL managers and their assistants heard the message the same way, right from the top... so that's why the meeting took place on a Sunday night at midnight, after all of the restaurants had closed.

This information could have been shared in a meeting room, but that would have been a horrible choice. This was a RALLY. There was food, drink, and PRIZES. And there were costumed characters all over the place. This was fun. But it was also extremely informative because the Phoenix market leaders knew that our employees would have to match the passion of the *Star* Wars fans that would be flooding into their restaurants (or so they hoped). That's why the senior leaders put on the costumes and showed what passion and commitment to this program looked like.

For me personally, this rally provided a great icebreaker when I visited each of the RGMs in their stores. And it set a great bar for me to try to exceed with all future interaction with the restaurant management teams in this market. I had to match the passion level of *Star Wars*, every time. Obi Wan is known as a wise character who provides sage advice—but on this day, Obi Wan was doing all of the learning.

Cube Tips

Sometimes inspiring others, motivating people, and driving culture requires you to step outside your comfort zone. I know the regional manager was not a big *Star Wars* fan, but he put on the Darth Vader costume and lived it—that's what passion and leadership are all about. Your reaction to new things will be modeled by the teams that count on your leadership. If you are passionate, they will be too. If you are skeptical, or act disinterested, they will do the same.

If you show an interest in another person's passion, the results will be significant. The managers that spent the time to understand the consumer promotion (and could speak basic *Star Wars* lingo) received repeat and loyal customers for life. The same will hold true as a manager and colleague if you show a sincere interest in the hobbies, pursuits, and personal passions of the people working around you inside their cubicles.

Chapter 28

THE MERGER OF MARKETING AND HUMOR

Passion in one area can often translate itself well in another area of one's life. My 20-plus years as a marketer have absolutely made me a better speaker, trainer, and comedian. Let's go INSIDE…

As a marketer, I have been unearthing insights about consumer behavior as it relates to products and services all of my life. Now, I am using that same lens of analyzing behavior, only in the speech or humor case, finding the underlying humor within that action. One of the best examples of a true human insight that is also very funny when analyzed bit by bit is the behavior that is associated with corporate conference calls, which I brought to life in Chapter 5.

A good marketer must also be a good writer…and a good speaker is nothing without the written word. So the ability to put succinct thoughts on paper to tell a story that will ultimately take the form of a TV commercial, a billboard, or a keynote speech overlap significantly. Marketers know every second of a TV commercial is precious, while speakers and comedians know that the fewer words it takes to pay off a joke or punch line, the better.

So, you never know how different expertise in your life will help you ooze more passion in a new pursuit.

Why was I always considered one of the best presenters where I worked? "Because he's a comedian" is the answer that was always given. While that is true on the surface, it masks my effort to get there. Yes, I enjoy speaking to a group of any size. But that has come from years of work, not because I happen to be funny. And that is a distinct difference.

When I coach people on their presentation styles, I urge them to find their comfort zone. And it does not have to be humor, or a big personality, that delivers. A quiet confidence is just as effective. But regardless of the style, the preparation is the key.

The hours I worked on difficult open mic night stages working on finding my ideal comedic style prepared me to be incredibly comfortable in the board room, on the national sales stage, or in the meeting room discussing a heated sales topic. The reality is that I have presented hundreds, if not thousands, of more hours than my colleagues. And that practice, that investment of time, makes me a top presenter. The fact that I am also funny is icing on the cake, and that is merely my style, not why I am good.

Cube Tips

Skills you have outside of the workplace can absolutely benefit your performance in the office. Your volunteer work can provide you with a chance to influence others, build teams, or drive morale. Recognize the crossover that exists and challenge yourself to improve your opportunity areas while maximizing what you are really good at. If you have mad math skills, helping out the church or nonprofit organization with maximizing their budgets and

investments can have a profound impact. Sometimes, you take your strengths for granted when they can really benefit others (including you!).

Chapter 29

FIND THE RIGHT RECOGNITION

Recognition can instantly put a smile on a face and lift the spirits of not just the recipient, but also an entire department. I have seen the good and bad sides of recognition and felt this was a fitting final paragraph. I believe strongly in the power of recognition. Let's go INSIDE…

The Cheese Head is a staple of Green Bay Packers fans. They wear them with pride. Their commitment to the team oozes right out of one of the "holes" in their beloved yellow foam headgear. It is a symbol that represents their Wisconsin roots and heritage. It represents the fans as much as it represents the team. It is uniquely their own. It is also the symbol of tremendous achievement at Pizza Hut.

As I stated earlier, Pizza Hut is one of the restaurants that make up YUM Brands, a company that truly believes in recognition. People are the key to the restaurant business and their leadership team knows it. So, celebrating wins and great work is infused throughout the organization.

It all starts at the top. David Novak, CEO of YUM Brands, has his own award. It is fun, it is coveted, and it reinforces the importance of recognition at all levels. His award is a large set of plastic teeth with legs (not kidding)—it's the "walk the talk" award that celebrates leadership. He knows the impact recognition can have on a company and makes sure it permeates the culture.

Having worked at Pizza Hut, I have seen this firsthand. Leaders at all levels had their own awards, with a variety of names and forms. From the "driving results" racecar to an electronic megaphone given out for great communication, these items were pervasive. But it was done right. No one ever thought, "Oh great, here comes another reward." We enjoyed reveling in the success of our colleagues, and the managers truly made the winner feel special.

These awards were also great because they were tied to specific business results. That takes the arbitrary out of the awards. Too many companies suck the passion out of their employees when they attempt to do just the opposite because awards are randomly given out. There is no cadence. There is no criteria. There is no reason. The senior leaders just get a sense that maybe morale isn't where it should be, so let's get the whole group together, give out some awards, and go bowling. Morale problem solved. Box checked. Uh, not so much—gutter ball.

Another thing that Pizza Hut leadership did brilliantly was recognize entire teams with their rewards. Too often, I have seen companies recognize merely the project leader (or one of the "high potential" leaders within a huge project that required the work of 10-plus people). Again, the idea to recognize comes from the right place. But then it fails miserably at arrival, as a huge project is the basis for an award, and a lone individual receives it.

You simply do not want your employees begrudging another person. But that is what happens when solo recognition happens within a large project. Do what Pizza Hut does: recognize the entire team. If it's a cross-functional project, haul the whole team up on stage for pictures (R&D, finance, innovation, marketing, PR, etc.).

That's what motivates—it's a great picture of passionate people that can inspire the entire organization.

That very same Packers Cheese Head plays a similarly important role at Pizza Hut. (Who knew foam formed in the shape of food acting as headgear could be so powerful?) It is the symbol of the top award at Pizza Hut, called "The Big Cheese" Award, given out by the CEO. I was lucky enough to receive one of these awards, on a large team for one of our successful pizza launches that takes the work of many to be successful. Fifteen of us were on stage, smiling, oozing passion...and wearing a Cheese Head.

Recognition is one of the best ways to manage a team. If you frequently provide impromptu recognition, especially if it is in front of a group, the receiver will feel inspired (and you will be seen as a person who truly cares about the people).

*BHT: Impromptu recognition can have the same effect as "no reason flowers"—one of the best moves any husband can make. All married men reading this right now on a day that is not their anniversary, wife's birthday, or Valentine's Day should put the book down (it's OK, you have my permission) and order a bouquet of her favorite flowers to arrive tomorrow, a day without significance—because you care. That piece of advice is my gift to you).

OK, you are back, and you probably feel really good about that online purchase. It feels good to recognize someone else. Not only will their morale soar, but so, too, should yours.

CuBe TiPs

Recognition is such a critical part of the culture of any workplace. Some, like Pizza Hut, do it really, really well. Make sure you follow their lead as you implement your own individual program or work within your company's plan. You do NOT have to be a manager to recognize the exemplary efforts of a work colleague.

To ensure that recognition has the desired, positive result, make sure you are consistent on timing, clear on the reason why an award was received, and are inclusive. If a whole team knocked a project out of the park, recognize all of them, not just one or two.

Finally, make an effort to consistently provide "no reason doughnuts" or other unexpected "thank yous" throughout the year that show your team you care. That investment in delicious, glazed baked goods will be returned 1,000 fold because your teams will want to continue to strive for perfection and make you proud.

Chapter 30

THE ROAD TO THIS BOOK

Without all of the workplaces and coworkers who have been a part of my life, this book would obviously not exist. My journey to bring all of the prior chapters to life on a stage was a challenging one. Here's how it started, with Cube Tips at the end for what I learned and how you can apply those tips to your life.

This cartoon started my comedy journey.

I sent this cartoon in response to an e-mail my colleague Allison sent me. Her response was, "You're so funny." And that was it. It was the proverbial "Tipping Point," Mr. Gladwell. I decided at that very moment that I was going to make every effort to get paid to be funny...but how?

After doing very little with that quest for two months, I arrived at the Cincinnati airport in Kentucky for my morning flight back to Dallas. And then the snow started, and the 9:00 a.m. flight became the 3:00, which became the 8:30 p.m. For those eight hours, I hunkered down outside of a gate number I do not remember, and I wrote while the flakes fell from the heavens.

I thought about all of the topics that I felt I could write with humor: tennis, football, and the workplace rose to the top. I settled on the office and wrote down everything I thought was funny (many of the concepts described in the prior chapters of this book came from a seedling at CVG that day). As each inch of snow fell, I was more engaged. I was on to something, but I just didn't know what.

At the end of eight hours, I had a list of ideas to write about. I tried to view each of these observations the way Jerry Seinfeld might have viewed a sock, a bowl of cereal, etc. I searched for the universal minutiae that everyone could relate to—I wanted to be the Seinfeld of the office.

Now what? The next step was to turn the lists into actual stand-up comedy bits. But how does one get into stand-up comedy? I was extremely comfortable on stage and had actually done one night of stand-up in college at Miami University.

*BHT: On this night, my future bride, the Lovely Deb Fleming, was in the audience and saw me perform for the first time (this was actually before the night we actually "met," ironically on a double date when we weren't each other's date). Each comic got five minutes, and I covered riveting material that included lightning bug sex ("Honey, lights are going off, this is amazing) and horseplay in swimming pools ("Can we get the saddle out of the deep end, please")—the crowd clapped, I was probably OK at best for a first timer.

So, that was dipping my toe into stand-up comedy. After that, I went to too many open mic nights and watched too many other comics, but I had one simple purpose: hone my craft.

Throughout this process, I was constantly writing. I knew how to write funny, so I just needed to find the most universally funny topics. I was getting so comfortable on stage and the laughs were coming, so I decided to make the gigantic leap from 10 minutes of material to a 75-minute, one-man show.

One of my favorite observations is the section about the universal love for denim. I thought that it would be the perfect open to a one-man show. Around this time, I was watching a college basketball game and watched the team take the floor by tearing away their sweats. An idea struck me... I needed a tear-away suit to reveal my denim. I'd never miss a Free Jeans Day if I had a tear-away suit.

So I Googled "tear-away suit," and nothing perfect was there. So I kept searching, and then I came upon a site that makes special clothing for elderly folks who have a harder time dressing themselves. And with the sweetest woman on the other end of the phone, I gave her MY pant and shirt sizes as I described how nice Grampa needed to look at a wedding in a few weeks.

The pants were perfect, Velcro-ed together and fit perfectly over my jeans. The dress shirt snapped down the back so I could just tear it free and go—high quality US craftsmanship. To see this suit in action, go to www.daveflemingspeaks.com.

The 75-minute, one-man show debuted in 2007. The tear-away suit was a massive hit, and people were paying money to see me perform. The laughs grew show by show. I had done it. I had figured out how to get paid to be funny.

Cube Tips

There are so many chances to show our creative side. Some people can draw, some can sing. In my case, I could always add a creative idea to a workplace problem. In my own personal situation, I needed a fun way to open my show. I have never sewed a day in my life, but I articulated exactly what I needed and I got the desired result. Challenge yourself to find additional ways to express your creativity and your ability to communicate on the job will be increased.

Finally, I often get asked, "How do you know what's funny?" How did I know? I trusted my personal judgment and observed the crazy things I saw unfolding all around me. I saw people freak out about an e-mail that was recalled—and I just knew it was funny. A win for my humorous stories as a speaker is not just the laughs but when I can hear people in the audience saying "that's so true." At that point I know I have touched on a relatable human emotion that also happened to be really funny.

THE FINAL CUBE TIP

I wrote this book because I truly felt that my view of the workplace could help others. I hope that is the case now that you have arrived here, at the end of the book. I hope you have laughed. But most importantly, I hope you have learned several new ideas that can help you make your workplace instantly more fun, more productive, and ultimately more rewarding.

===== CuBe TiPs =====

Laugh. Every day.

Made in the USA
Charleston, SC
09 August 2015